The Easy Gourmet

Hearty Winter Stews & Casseroles

SAFEWAY

Canada Safeway Limited 🍁

EILEEN DWILLIES
ANN MERLING
ANGELA NILSEN
EDENA SHELDON

OPUS PRODUCTIONS INC.
VANCOUVER

Published and produced for Canada Safeway Limited by
Opus Productions Inc.
1128 Homer Street
Vancouver, B.C., Canada
V6B 2X6

Canadian Cataloguing in Publication Data
    Main entry under title:
    Hearty winter stews and casseroles

            (The Easy Gourmet ; v.3)
            Includes index.
            ISBN 0-921926-02-2

        1. Stews. 2. Casserole cookery. I. Series.
        TX693.H42 1989   641.8'23   C89-091355-2

Corporate Consultant: Mark McCurdy, Palmer Jarvis Advertising
Editor: Mary Schendlinger
Production Manager: Orest Kinasevych
Designers: Tim Kelly, David Counsell
Recipe Coordinator: Eileen Dwillies
Food Stylist: Edena Sheldon
Test Kitchen Manager and Food Stylist Assistant: Arline Smith
Test Kitchen Staff: Kathy Alexander, Marti Bjorndahl, Margot Brown,
                    Fran Donis, Janet Dwillies, Joanne Facchin,
                    Arlyne Ledingham, Judy Lye, Jennie Meier,
                    Joyce Miller, Marge Milne, Pat Orr, Barb Resvick,
                    Alison Sclater

Produced exclusively on the IBM Personal Publishing System and
    IBM PS/2 Personal Systems.

On the cover: Creole Jambalaya (p. 68).

Printed in Canada by Friesen Printers.

"The Easy Gourmet" TM

TABLE OF CONTENTS

About the authors

Eileen Dwillies, whose recipes and articles have been published in *Western Living, Canadian Living* and other Canadian periodicals, also works as a food stylist for print and television, and teaches cooking in her home. Ann Merling is a microwave consultant, teacher and home economist whose extensive experience includes twelve years working with microwave manufacturers and teaching microwave cooking to consumers. Angela Nilsen, a home economist, food stylist and cooking instructor, has written numerous recipes and articles for publications in Europe and North America, and was a food writer with the *Vancouver Sun* for seven years. Edena Sheldon's food features and recipes have appeared for U.S. magazines, newspapers and cookbooks including *Bon Appétit, Sunset* and the *Los Angeles Times*. More recently, her work has been published in Canada, in the *Canada Cooks!* series and in *Western Living Magazine*. She enjoys a continuing reputation as a food and prop stylist.

All four authors bring to the recipes their extensive food writing experience, the unique influences of their world travels, and most of all their appreciation of the cooking traditions of Western Canada, where all of them make their home.

About the recipes

Every recipe in this book is carefully and thoroughly kitchen-tested, by a team that includes both new and experienced cooks.

For convenience in shopping and measuring, we "rounded off" in listing the metric quantities of recipe ingredients; 1 lb. is converted as 500 g, rather than the technically correct 454 g; 1/2 lb. is shown as 250 g, and so on.

All of the microwave recipes were tested in microwave ovens of 700 watts, so if yours is in the 600 watt range, add 15% to the suggested cooking times. And remember to start with the minimum suggested time and add extra if necessary—every microwave, like every convection oven, is unique.

We used large eggs and whole milk unless specified otherwise, and we used unsalted butter without exception. When you cook with herbs, remember that dried herbs are much more concentrated than fresh ones, so if you substitute dried herbs for fresh, use one-third the amount. When a recipe calls for wine, liqueur, or other alcoholic beverage, there is usually a substitute ingredient listed. There are non-alcoholic cooking wines and liqueurs available, but unless the recipe specifically calls for them, we did not use them, as their salt content is quite high.

When preparing soups, stews, or any recipe containing acidic ingredients (tomatoes, citrus juice, vinegar, wine, etc.), we recommend the use of a non-reactive pot or pan such as stainless steel, enamel-coated cast-iron, porcelain, or glass. See our notes on cookware, page 7.

INTRODUCTION

Welcome to *The Easy Gourmet: Hearty Winter Stews & Casseroles*, the third in Canada Safeway's series of four cookbooks created to celebrate our Sixtieth Anniversary.

In this volume you will find a cornucopia of recipes for hearty meals, casseroles, stews, soups, and breads—all designed to satisfy the more robust appetites that come with the cooler autumn weather. The book has been written by the four top food writers who created the mouth-watering main dish recipes in Volume One, *Entrées: The Main Event*, and the outdoor cooking ideas in Volume Two, *Summer Salads and Barbecue Cookouts*.

Some of the recipes in this volume, as in all of the books in the series, are designed for preparation in the microwave. Look for the special microwave symbol M.

Autumn means brisk weather, changing colours, the excitement of back-to-school—and most of all, a time to come inside and gather round the dinner table for a warm, fragrant meal with family and friends. So open this book and rediscover the joys of time-tested hearty meals—Best-Ever Beet Borscht, Classic Meat Loaf, or Molasses Baked Beans with Spareribs—or a 1980s-style creation like Tarragon Pork Pie, Mariners' Stew, or Party Time Chorizo Chili. Our recipe for wonderful cool-weather eating? Take this inspiring and wide-ranging collection of harvest-time one-dish meals, add the authors' expertise and love of the world's great cuisine, mix in our careful kitchen-testing of each recipe. Sprinkle liberally with Safeway's wide selection of high-quality fresh and packaged foods, and the fully experienced and very helpful experts who staff every department in the store. Serve, and enjoy!

Hearty Meals

The first section in the book is devoted to hot, filling, stick-to-your-ribs main dishes designed especially for cool weather. They range from fish and poultry dishes, prepared quickly and served at once, to robust entrées that need longer cooking and can be made ahead. Meat, vegetable, and legume (lentils and dried beans and peas) dishes can be refrigerated for up to 4 days, ground meat dishes for up to 3 days, and poultry for up to 2 days. Entrées made of fresh seafood are best served the same day.

Casseroles

One-dish meals are not only delicious opportunities to combine your favourite autumn flavours, they are a real boon to the busy cook—one pan goes from oven to table and is often a complete balanced meal. Many of the casseroles in this section can be prepared ahead and refrigerated. Watch for the authors' advice on dishes that are ideal make-aheads, and plan to reheat and serve the casserole within 2 days. If you're "cooking ahead" on the weekend, or if you have leftovers, remember that casseroles freeze very well. Wrap the whole casserole or individual portions in freezer quality foil or plastic wrap and reheat in the oven or microwave.

Stews

Like many of the hearty meals in this book, stews are perfect for the weekend chef. So take your time on a big pot of your favourite stew and refrigerate or freeze it for weekday dinners—the flavours just get better and better! Remember that refrigerated meat, vegetable, and legume stews are best served within 4 days of preparation, ground meat dishes within 3 days, and poultry within 2 days. Seafood stews are best served as soon as they are cooked.

Soups

Soups, chowders, bisques, broths—they're all here, in a section devoted to the classic comfort food that many people believe is also a cure for the common cold! Many of the recipes here start with beef or chicken stock, and we have included recipes for homemade versions of these, but canned stock is a great convenience food short-cut. Other soups in this section, such as Favourite Scotch Broth and Hearty Smoked Ham and Pea Soup, are started from scratch and make their own delicious broth as they simmer. All of the meat-based soups are as good or better when made ahead, because their flavours blend over time and you can skim them when cool. Store them in the refrigerator for up to 4 days. Soups with a milk or cream base and soups that call for seafood are generally prepared much more quickly than meat-based soups, and are best served right after they are prepared.

Breads

Surely the most soul-warming accompaniment to any of the hot, wholesome entrées in this book—and indeed, to any meal of the day—is a pan of fresh bread or muffins. The trick to light, perfectly-textured quick breads is to mix the wet ingredients into the dry ones quickly, just until the flour is moistened, and bake immediately.

Slow-Cooking

Many of the hearty meat entrées, stews, and soups in this volume call for slow-cooking on low heat, in the oven or on top of the stove.

The slow-cooking method of meal preparation is a joy to the busy cook who looks for the very best in flavour, nutrition, and economy. The long cooking time allows the flavours of the ingredients to develop and blend together—with the added bonus of the fragrant aromas that please everyone in the house!—and for most of the recipes in this book, there is little attention required during the simmering period. The best thing about many of these soups, stews, and hearty meals is that they can be made ahead and reheated in a hurry after a busy day.

Stewing

Stew meat is cut in smaller pieces than braised or pot roasted meat, and stewing is simply covering or nearly covering the meat with liquid (water, broth, or gravy) before simmering in a tightly-covered pan.

Braising or Pot Roasting

In this method, a large piece of meat, such as a whole roast, is browned in butter or other fat and cooked with a small amount of liquid in a tightly-covered pan.

Cookware

Many of the recipes for hearty meals, stews, and soups call for large, deep pots. These come in many varieties, including the following.

Stainless steel

Stainless steel is wonderful for most cooking because it is sturdy and heavy, does not react chemically with foods, and stays bright and shiny. The best kind of cookware is stainless steel with a bottom made of a "sandwich" of other metals that conduct heat more rapidly.

Cast-iron

This metal works well because it is heavy and unbreakable, and it spreads heat slowly and evenly. If you use cast-iron pots, keep them seasoned, and don't let food sit in them—they rust rapidly. Enamel-coated cast-iron is easier to care for, and though it tends to chip over time, its qualities are not affected. Food may be stored in the enamel-coated variety, and because of the bright colours, these pans are ideal for freezer to oven to table dinners.

Earthenware

Earthenware vessels work well for long cooking at low temperatures because they transmit heat quite slowly but stay hot once they are heated through. Foods cooked in earthenware pots need frequent stirring to prevent scorching, and earthenware is breakable. Follow the manufacturer's directions if you are using earthenware for oven stews—the cooking time may be different than with metal—and check whether your earthenware needs seasoning before it is used.

Aluminum

Durable and lightweight, aluminum is a good conductor of heat and a very practical cookware material. Because of their sensitivity to heat change (they are usually very thin), aluminum pots are good but not recommended for slow-cooking, as food burns easily when cooked over a long period. Some foods (tomato-based sauces and soups, vinegar, citrus juice, and other acidic foods) react chemically with aluminum and can discolour food and change its taste. Do not store food in aluminum pans, and it is best not to allow food to stand in them longer than a few minutes.

Clay Bakers

Clay bakers are like earthenware but can tolerate higher temperatures. They are soaked in water before using, and they produce tender meat or poultry with little added fat or liquid required. Like earthenware pots, clay bakers can require different cooking periods than metal pots, so check the directions.

Electric Crock-Pots

Designed especially for slow-cooking, these are wonderful appliances because the heat can be set very low. You can get everything ready in the morning and come home to dinner! We did not use crock-pots in our test kitchens, so if you like this method of preparing stews and pot roasts, adapt the recipes according to the manufacturer's instructions.

HEARTY MEALS

In this section, you will find recipes for soul-warming main dishes created to satisfy on cool fall evenings. There are tempting versions of old favourites—Spiced Pot Roast with Winter Vegetables, Tarragon-Sour Cream Chicken, Chunky Beef and Bean Burritos—and some exciting new ideas like Greek-Style Skillet Prawns with Feta and Game Hens with Apples and Mustard Cream Sauce.

SPICED POT ROAST WITH WINTER VEGETABLES

This recipe, a variation on the classic, is best prepared ahead. What a boon to busy households—a complete dinner on hand that needs only a quick reheat. Serve with wide egg noodles drizzled with the pan gravy. Serves 8-10.

3 cups	dry red wine	750 mL
1/4 cup	olive oil	60 mL
1	onion, chopped	1
1/4 cup	red wine vinegar	60 mL
2	cloves garlic, slivered	2
1/2 tsp.	*each* ground cloves, cinnamon, nutmeg, coriander, thyme, ginger, and black pepper	2 mL
	grated rind of 1 orange	
3	bay leaves	3
1	6 lb. (3 kg) bottom round roast or top round roast	1
2 tbsp.	*each* butter and olive oil	30 mL
1	large onion, halved and thinly sliced	1
	salt and pepper to taste	
2 tsp.	brown sugar	10 mL
2 cups	rich beef stock	500 mL
6 tbsp.	ketchup	90 mL
1 lb.	carrots, peeled and cut into 2 inch (5 cm) pieces	500 g
1 lb.	rutabagas, peeled and cut into 2 inch (5 cm) cubes	500 g
1 lb.	parsnips, peeled and cut in half lengthwise	500 g
3 tbsp.	*each* softened butter and flour (optional)	45 mL
	minced fresh parsley	

Combine the red wine, 1/4 cup (60 mL) olive oil, chopped onion, vinegar, garlic, cloves, cinnamon, nutmeg, coriander, thyme, ginger, pepper, orange rind, and bay leaves. Marinate the roast in this mixture 24 hours, turning several times.

Remove the beef from marinade, reserving and straining the marinade. Heat the 2 tbsp. (30 mL) butter and olive oil in a heavy Dutch oven over medium heat. Add the onions and sauté, stirring, until golden. Pat the roast dry and add it to the pot. Increase the heat to high, and brown the roast on all sides, seasoning with salt and pepper. Sprinkle with brown sugar as the meat browns. Add the beef stock and strained marinade to the pot, and bring the liquid to a simmer. Add the ketchup, stir to blend, and cover the roast. Simmer 2 1/2 hours, or until the meat is almost tender.

Add to the simmering liquid the prepared carrots, rutabagas, parsnips, and onions. Cover and simmer 30 minutes. Remove from heat, uncover, and allow to cool to room temperature. Cover and chill for 1 to 3 days.

To serve, skim the fat from the top of the roast. Place the pot over low heat and reheat slowly for 1 hour. Lift out the roast and set it on a warmed platter. Lift out the vegetables with a slotted spoon. If the gravy needs thickening, work together the softened butter and flour and add it to the simmering gravy, bit by bit, to thicken to the desired consistency. Slice the pot roast, spoon gravy over the slices, and serve surrounded by the vegetables. Sprinkle with minced parsley and serve.

EW ENGLAND CORNED BEEF AND VEGETABLES

With this unique recipe for the classic boiled dinner, there is no guesswork on timing—everything simmers to tender perfection in the fragrant poaching stock. Try this glazed corned beef version, served with an array of fresh winter vegetables, and offer a variety of mustards and a horseradish-spiked whipped cream as condiments. Home-baked biscuits and a crock of butter complete this warming dinner for a blustery winter's evening. Serves 6-8.

1	4-5 lb. (2-2.5 kg) corned beef brisket	1
1 tbsp.	*each* Kosher salt and whole black peppercorns	15 mL
2	bay leaves	2
2/3 cup + 1 tbsp.	brown sugar, packed	165 mL
8	small turnips	8
4	rutabagas (Swedes or yellow turnips)	4
8	medium onions	8
8	carrots	8
8	red-skinned potatoes	8
8	small leeks	8
1	head green cabbage	1
1/2 tsp.	ground cloves	2 mL
1 tsp.	dry English-style mustard	5 mL
3 tbsp.	sherry (optional)	45 mL
	assorted sharp, sweet, honey, and grainy mustards	
	Horseradish-Spiked Whipped Cream (recipe follows)	

Place the corned beef in a deep stock pot. Cover with water and add the salt, peppercorns, bay leaves, and 1 tbsp. (15 mL) of the brown sugar. Bring the liquid to a simmer, partially cover the pot, and simmer until the meat is just fork-tender, about 3 hours.

While it simmers, get the vegetables ready for cooking. Wash the turnips and trim the tops off, leaving 1 inch (2.5 cm) of green stems intact. Peel and halve the rutabagas. Peel the brown skins from the whole onions, leaving the root and pointed stem intact. Pare the carrots, leaving 1 inch (2.5 cm) of green stem attached. Scrub the red potatoes and peel a 1/2 inch (1 cm) band around the centre of each to prevent bursting. Wash the leeks well, trim, and discard the root ends and leathery green stems. Wash the cabbage and cut into 8 wedges.

Gently lift the meat from the pot and drain, reserving the stock. Place the meat in a baking dish.

Heat the oven to 350°F (180°C). Mix together the remaining brown sugar, cloves, dry mustard, and sherry. Spread this paste over top of the cooked brisket. Pour 2 tbsp. (30 mL) of the corned beef stock into the bottom of the baking dish to prevent the meat from drying out. Bake the beef, uncovered, 30-45 minutes, or until golden brown on top.

While the beef is baking, bring the corned beef stock to a gentle boil. Add the turnips, rutabagas, onions, carrots, and potatoes. Cook uncovered 15 minutes. Add the leeks and cook 10 minutes longer. Add the cabbage and cook 7-8 minutes longer. Remove the vegetables from the liquid and drain.

Slice the glazed corned beef in thick or thin slices and arrange it on a large, warmed platter. Surround it with the cooked vegetables. Spoon a bit of the poaching liquid over the vegetables. Serve at once, accompanied by the mustards and Horseradish-Spiked Whipped Cream.

HORSERADISH-SPIKED WHIPPED CREAM

2 cups	whipping cream, chilled	500 mL
3 tbsp.	prepared horseradish	45 mL
	(bottled, not creamed style)	
1 tsp.	sugar	5 mL
1 tsp.	white vinegar	5 mL
	salt and white pepper to taste	

Combine the cream, horseradish, and sugar. Whip the mixture until medium-stiff billowy peaks form (do not whip dry). Add the vinegar and season delicately with salt and white pepper. Serve chilled with the sliced corned beef.

CALVES LIVER STEAK WITH RED ONION MARMALADE

This elegant presentation turns a humble, often neglected meat into true dining fare. Sautéed to a rosy turn with herbs and pepper, the tender liver steaks are wonderful with mashed potatoes and fresh spinach tossed with toasted pine nuts. Serves 4.

2 tbsp.	olive oil	30 mL
2-3 tbsp.	butter	30-45 mL
1 1/2 lbs.	calves liver, cut 1/4 inch (6 mm) thick and patted dry	750 g
	salt and coarsely ground black pepper to taste	
1 tsp.	*each* dried rosemary (crumbled) and dried thyme	5 mL
	Red Onion Marmalade (recipe follows)	

In a large, heavy non-stick skillet, heat the oil and butter over medium-high heat until bubbly. Allow the foam to subside and quickly add the liver steaks. Sear on one side 3-4 minutes, seasoning with salt, pepper, and herbs. Turn the steaks, sear the other side, and season. Cook the steaks until crusty and browned on the outside, rosy-pink and juicy on the inside. When pressed, the meat will feel just firmed near the top, with a slightly resilient centre. Transfer the liver to warmed plates and serve at once with a generous spoonful of Red Onion Marmalade.

RED ONION MARMALADE

1 tbsp.	olive oil	15 mL
2 tbsp.	butter	30 mL
4 cups	thinly sliced red onion	1 L
1 tbsp.	sugar	15 mL
1 tbsp.	balsamic vinegar *or* red wine vinegar	15 mL
2 tbsp.	port	30 mL
	salt and pepper to taste	

Heat a deep saucepan over medium heat. Add the oil and butter, and heat to foaming. Add the onions, toss to coat, and sauté slowly until softened and wilted. Increase the heat to medium-high and continue to cook the onions, sprinkling them with the sugar and vinegar, until they carmelize, about 15 minutes. Add the port and increase the heat to high. Cook, stirring, 3-4 minutes to evaporate the alcohol. The finished marmalade should be condensed, glossy, and syrupy, with most of the juices absorbed. Season lightly with salt and pepper to taste. Remove from the heat, cool to just barely warm or room temperature, and serve.

UICK FRUIT'N'GINGER POT ROAST

Tasting is believing in this deliciously different pot roast—the flavours of ginger, tea, prunes, olives, and rich beef stock combine beautifully for a unique and hearty main dish. Serve it accompanied by creamy mashed potatoes and microwaved broccoli or green beans. Serves 6-8.

1 tsp.	*each* salt, pepper, and ground ginger	5 mL
1	3-4 lb. (1.5-2 kg) chuck or rolled rump roast	1
2 cups	weak tea	500 mL
12	pitted prunes, quartered	12
2 tbsp.	butter or oil	30 mL
2	large onions, chopped	2
1	clove garlic, chopped	1
1/2 cup	burgundy wine or beef stock	125 mL
4 tbsp.	all-purpose flour	60 mL
1	10 oz. (284 mL) can sliced mushrooms, drained	1
1/2 cup	pitted green olives, sliced	125 mL

Mix together the salt, pepper, and ginger and rub the mixture over the surface of the meat. Place the roast in a microproof casserole dish.

Heat the tea on HIGH 100% power until hot. Add the prunes and set aside.

Place the butter, onions, and garlic in a microproof dish. Cover and microwave on HIGH 100% power 4-6 minutes until the onion is soft, stirring once during the cooking time. Blend in the wine and pour the mixture over the meat. Cover and microwave on MEDIUM 50% power, allowing 24-27 minutes per pound (500 g) of meat. Halfway through the cooking time, turn the meat over and baste with sauce.

Place the flour in a small bowl. Drain the tea over the flour and blend until smooth. Add the prunes, mushrooms, and olives to the meat. Add the flour and tea mixture. Cover and microwave on MEDIUM 50% power 5-10 minutes until the mixture is thickened slightly. Slice the meat, top with the sauce, and serve.

OM'S BEST MEAT LOAF WITH GARLICKY POTATOES

Food trends come and go, but somehow meat loaf keeps its status as a good, tasty, versatile dish. Here is a great one, basic and hearty, served deliciously warm from the oven with garlic-spiked mashed potatoes and fresh broccoli. And there's a bonus—the meat loaf is just as good served cold in sandwiches the next day. Makes 1 large meat loaf.

1	medium onion, minced	1
6	slices bacon, diced	6
2	cloves garlic, minced	2
1 1/2 lbs.	lean ground beef or a combination of ground beef, veal, and pork	750 g
2	eggs, lightly beaten	2
4 tbsp.	bottled horseradish	60 mL
1/2 cup	old-fashioned rolled oats	125 mL
1/3 cup	grated Parmesan cheese	75 mL
1 tsp.	*each* salt, black pepper, celery seed, dill seed, and dried thyme	5 mL
1/3 cup	tomato sauce or ketchup	75 mL
2 tbsp.	brown sugar, packed	30 mL

Sauté the onion with the bacon and garlic until golden. With your hands, or in a large bowl of an electric mixer fitted with a dough hook, gently combine the meat, onion-bacon-garlic mixture, eggs, horseradish, oats, Parmesan, salt, pepper, celery seed, dill seed, and thyme. Knead gently but thoroughly until the mixture is very light and fluffy. Heat the oven to 350°F (180°C).

Pack the mixture into a 2 quart (2 L) rectangular glass loaf pan, levelling the top gently. Spoon the tomato sauce over top of the loaf and sprinkle with the brown sugar.

Bake the meat loaf in the centre of the oven for 1 1/2 hours. Let it cool 30 minutes before slicing and serving warm. You can also cool the meat loaf completely, cover tightly in plastic wrap, and chill overnight. Using a thin knife, slice the loaf into thin slices for sandwiches.

GARLICKY MASHED POTATOES

Serves 4.

4	large baking potatoes, each about 3/4 lb. (375 g), scrubbed in cold water and dried	4
1 cup	milk	250 mL
1/3-1/2 cup	half-and-half cream	75-125 mL
2	large cloves garlic, crushed	2
4 tbsp.	butter	60 mL
1/3 cup	finely minced green onion (white and tender green part only)	75 mL
	salt and freshly ground black pepper to taste	

Bake the potatoes in a 375°F (190°C) oven about 1 hour, or until the skins are crisp and the insides are soft when squeezed. Bring to a simmer the milk, cream, garlic, butter, and scallions, melting the butter completely. While the potatoes are hot, scoop out the flesh and force it through a ricer, or mash with the back of a fork. Add almost all the warm liquid, incorporating the potatoes so they are light, creamy, and fluffy. Add the last bit of liquid, a few drops at a time, to reach the desired consistency. Season to taste with salt and black pepper. Serve at once, piping hot, in a warmed bowl.

MEXICAN OLIVE-RAISIN MEAT LOAF

Simple to assemble and easy to bake, this meat loaf is Mexican inspired, full of spicy seasonings and studded with green olives and raisins to add colour. Serve warm with Spanish rice, hot corn bread, fresh braised zucchini, and a crisp, leafy green salad. Makes one large meat loaf.

2 lbs.	lean ground beef	1 kg
1	medium onion, finely minced	1
2	cloves garlic, crushed	2
1	1.25 oz. (38 g) package taco seasoning mix	1
1	8 oz. (255 mL) bottle prepared red taco sauce	1
2	eggs, lightly beaten	2
1/2 cup	fresh bread crumbs	125 mL
1/2 cup	grated Parmesan cheese	125 mL
1 tbsp.	dried oregano, crumbled	15 mL
2/3 cup	sliced pimiento-stuffed green olives	150 mL
1/2 cup	dried currants or raisins, soaked	125 mL
	15 minutes in warm water to cover and drained	
2 tsp.	salt	10 mL
1 tsp.	black pepper	5 mL

With your hands, or in a large bowl of an electric mixer fitted with a dough hook, mix the ground beef with the onion, garlic, seasoning mix, two-thirds of the taco sauce, the eggs, all but 1 tbsp. (15 mL) of the crumbs, all but 1 tbsp. (15 mL) of the Parmesan, the oregano, olives, drained currants, salt, and pepper. Knead gently but thoroughly until the mixture is very light and fluffy. Heat the oven to 350°F (180°C).

Pack the mixture into a 2 quart (2 L) rectangular glass loaf pan, levelling the top gently. Spread the remaining taco sauce over top, and sprinkle evenly with the reserved bread crumbs and Parmesan. Bake in the centre of the oven 1 hour and 20 minutes. Set the meat loaf on a wire rack to cool for at least 45 minutes before serving.

The Easy Gourmet features a photograph of this recipe on page 35.

Opposite: Sauerkraut Choucroute with Parsleyed Potatoes (p. 26).

CLASSIC MEAT LOAF

This family favourite is always easy, always right. Mix up the classic loaf, or dress it up with a filling of sautéed spinach, mushrooms and onions, or chopped hard-boiled egg, or mashed cooked carrots. Serve steamed green beans, mashed potatoes, and thick steamy gravy, and you have an irresistible "diner dinner"! Makes four 2-inch (5 cm) slices.

1 lb.	meat loaf mix (a combination of ground beef, ground pork and ground veal, or medium ground beef)	500 g
1	egg, slightly beaten	1
1	small onion, diced	1
2 tbsp.	chopped herbs, such as parsley, oregano, and chives	30 mL
2 tbsp.	fine or coarse dry bread crumbs	30 mL
pinch	*each* salt and pepper	pinch
dash	bottled hot pepper sauce	dash

Heat the oven to 350°F (180°C).

In a medium bowl, mix all the ingredients together. Press firmly into a 4 x 8 x 3 inch (10 x 20 x 8 cm) loaf pan or a 1 quart (1 L) casserole, filling any cavities. If you are preparing a filling, layer half the meat mixture in the pan, spread over it the prepared filling of your choice, and press the remaining meat on firmly to fill any cavities.

Bake until the top is crusty and dark brown, about 50-60 minutes.

CHUNKY BEEF AND BEAN BURRITOS

Mexican food is high on everyone's list of favourites, and chunky filled burritos are one of the reasons. Easy to fix and economical, the delicious filling may be prepared 2 days ahead, ready to reheat at a moment's notice for a great after-football supper. Serve in warmed flour tortillas, each topped with a dollop of sour cream and avocado guacamole, and a spoonful of fresh red salsa. Makes 10 burritos.

2 tbsp.	corn oil	30 mL
2 lbs.	lean ground beef	1 kg
1	large onion, diced	1
1	*each* green and red bell pepper, diced	1
2	cloves garlic, crushed	2
1 tbsp.	*each* brown sugar and red wine vinegar	15 mL
1 tsp.	*each* ground cumin, cinnamon, allspice, salt, black pepper, and oregano	5 mL
2 tbsp.	chili powder	30 mL
1	14 oz. (398 mL) can tomatoes, broken up into coarse dice (or use canned stewed tomatoes)	1
1/3 cup	*each* dried currants and pine nuts	75 mL
2	14 oz. (398 mL) cans Mexican-style refried beans	2
10	10 inch (25 cm) flour tortillas (one 15 oz.(425g) package)	10
1 cup	sour cream	250 mL
	Fresh Avocado Guacamole (recipe follows)	
1 pint	fresh red tomato salsa	500 mL

Prepare the filling up to 2 days before serving. Heat the corn oil in a large skillet over medium-high heat and add the ground beef. Sauté, breaking up the beef with a spoon, until it is no longer pink. Drain off excess fat. Add the onions, peppers, and garlic, and continue to sauté until the vegetables are softened. Stir in the brown sugar, vinegar, cumin, cinnamon, allspice, salt, pepper, oregano, and chili powder. Heat the mixture until it is bubbly and cook 3-4 minutes to blend the spices into the meat. Stir in the tomatoes and their liquid, increase the heat, and cook uncovered so that the mixture thickens and the juices are re-absorbed. Stir in the currants and pine nuts, bring the mixture to a simmer, partially cover, and cook 15-20 minutes. Taste and correct for seasonings, remove from the heat, and set aside.

Heat the refried beans in a skillet or saucepan. Wrap the tortillas in foil and place in a heated 350°F (180°C) oven for 15 minutes.

To assemble each burrito, place a heaping spoonful of refried beans down the centre of one warmed tortilla. Add about 1/3 cup (75 mL) meat filling down the centre. Roll up the filled tortilla and place it on a warmed plate, seam side down. Garnish each filled burrito with a dollop of sour cream, a spoonful of Fresh Avocado Guacamole, and fresh red salsa. Serve at once.

FRESH AVOCADO GUACAMOLE

2	very ripe large avocados	2
2 tbsp.	fresh lime juice	30 mL
1 tsp.	salt	5 mL
1/4 tsp.	cayenne pepper	1 mL
	several dashes bottled hot pepper sauce	
4 tbsp.	finely minced onion	60 mL
3 tbsp.	finely minced fresh cilantro	45 mL
1	small clove garlic, crushed (optional)	1
1-2	finely minced jalapeño chiles or	1-2
	2 tbsp. (30 mL) canned diced roasted chiles	
2	small Roma tomatoes, finely diced	2

Halve, pit and peel the avocados, and mash with the back of a fork to a chunky purée (do not use a food processor). Add all remaining ingredients and blend with a fork. Cover tightly with plastic wrap and chill until ready to serve.

Note: The freezer section offers a wonderful prepared guacamole if you don't have time to make your own. Simply thaw, stir, and serve.

SAUCE BOLOGNESE

From the town of Bologna in Italy, this rich, meaty sauce is sometimes called a ragu, which means "to excite the appetite." It is famous the world over, although the Bolognese claim no one can make it like they can. The long simmering time is essential for the best flavour, so make it on the weekend and freeze it for later use. The recipe will double or triple quite well. It's great over tortellini, wonderful in lasagne and excellent with any macaroni-type pasta. Try it with fresh green fettuccini. Serves 4 (makes 4-5 cups [1-1.25 L]).

1/2	medium onion	1/2
3 tbsp.	olive oil	45 mL
3 tbsp.	butter	45 mL
1	clove garlic, minced	1
1	stalk celery, minced	1
1	carrot, finely chopped	1
1 lb.	lean ground beef	500 g
	salt to taste	
1 cup	dry white wine or chicken stock or canned broth	250 mL
1/2 cup	milk	125 mL
pinch	nutmeg	pinch
pinch	freshly ground black pepper	pinch
2	14 oz. (398 mL) cans Roma tomatoes, with juice, roughly chopped	2
1 cup	tomato sauce (optional)	250 mL
1 lb.	fresh green fettuccini or the pasta of your choice	500 g
	Parmesan cheese for garnish	

Use a deep, heavy, cast-iron casserole or pot to keep the sauce from reducing too quickly. Put in it the chopped onion, oil, and butter and heat on medium-high heat until the onion is just translucent. Add the garlic and cook for 1 minute. Reduce the heat and add the celery and carrot. Cook for 2 minutes.

Add the ground beef, crumbling it in the pot. Add a pinch of salt, stir and cook only until the meat has lost its raw look. Do not brown. Add the wine and turn up the heat to medium-high. Cook, stirring, until evaporated. Reduce the heat to medium and add the milk, nutmeg, and pepper. Cook, stirring occasionally, until the milk has evaporated.

Add the tomatoes and stir well. When the tomatoes have started to boil, turn down the heat to the lowest setting and cook slowly, uncovered, stirring occasionally, until the sauce is thick and rich. Taste for seasonings and add more salt, pepper and nutmeg if desired. This takes about 1-2 hours, depending upon how low you can turn your stove burner. The sauce will look very meaty and taste wonderful. It can be made ahead to this point.

Cool the sauce and skim off any extra fat. When ready to serve, reheat to boiling and cook on a gentle simmer for 10 minutes or until hot. For a sauce richer in tomato, stir in the tomato sauce.

Fill a large pot with water and when it boils add the pasta. Cook al dente (just firm to the bite). Drain it in a colander or strainer. Do not rinse. Shake well to remove water. Divide the pasta among the serving plates and spoon over a generous serving of the Sauce Bolognese. Sprinkle with Parmesan cheese and serve immediately.

TRIO OF HEARTY SKILLET-GRILLED SANDWICHES

Remember when Mom used to make old-fashioned grilled cheese sandwiches in a beloved, well-used skillet, all toasty and buttery and crispy on the outside, with melted cheese running out with the first delicious bite? Well, here they are again, revisited with an update—new, fun, and utterly delicious fillings, quickly done in the skillet. Serve as a hearty lunch, or at supper accompanied by a steaming bowl of one of the excellent soups in this book, or any time the mood strikes! Each recipe makes 1 sandwich.

SKILLET-GRILLED RUEBEN

1 tbsp.	*each* mayonnaise and sharp mustard	15 mL
2	slices rye bread (seeded or plain), crusts on, 1/2 inch (1 cm) thick	2
2	1 oz. (30 g) slices Swiss or Muenster cheese	2
2 oz.	corned beef, thinly sliced	60 g
2 tbsp.	deli-style sauerkraut	30 mL
	softened butter	
	deli-style dill pickles	
	horseradish	

Combine the mayonnaise and mustard, and spread on one side of each slice of bread. Layer on the cheese and corned beef, tucking the sauerkraut in the middle, and ending with cheese. Top with the remaining slice of bread, and press gently together. Spread softened butter evenly over the outsides of the filled sandwich. Heat a non-stick or heavily seasoned skillet over medium heat 2-3 minutes. Place the sandwich in the skillet (it should sizzle at once) and grill 3-4 minutes until rich golden brown. Turn the sandwich carefully with a wide metal spatula, and grill the remaining side. Serve at once, hot from the skillet, with big dill pickles and creamed horseradish on the side.

SKILLET-GRILLED HAM ' N ' CHEESE

1 tbsp.	mayonnaise	15 mL
2	slices firm homestyle white bread, crusts on, 3/4 inch (2 cm) thick	2
2	1 oz. (30 g) slices cheddar, Swiss, or jack cheese	2
2 oz.	Black Forest ham, sliced thin	60 g
	softened butter	
	honey mustard	

Spread mayonnaise on one side of each slice of bread, right to the edges. Layer on the cheese and ham, ending with cheese. Top with the remaining slice of bread, and press together. Spread softened butter evenly over the outsides of the sandwich. Heat a non-stick or heavily seasoned skillet over medium heat 2-3 minutes. Grill the sandwich (it should sizzle as soon as it is placed in the skillet) 3-4 minutes until rich golden brown. Turn the sandwich with a wide metal spatula, and grill the remaining side. Serve at once, hot from the skillet, with honey mustard on the side.

CROQUE MADAME

1/3 cup	herbed cream cheese, softened	75 mL
1 tbsp.	mayonnaise	15 mL
1 tbsp.	snipped chives or parsley	15 mL
2	slices firm homestyle white bread or French bread, crusts removed, cut diagonally 3/4 inch (2 cm) thick	2
2 oz.	smoked turkey or chicken breast, thinly sliced	60 g
5	cooked asparagus spears, tip-ends, cut to fit length of bread	5
	softened butter	
	cranberry relish	

Combine the softened cream cheese and mayonnaise, and add the chives. Mix well to combine and spread lightly over one side of each slice of bread. Layer on the sliced turkey, tucking the asparagus spears in the centre, and binding with a bit of the cream cheese mixture. End with turkey. Top with the remaining slice of bread, and press gently together. Spread softened butter evenly over the outsides of the sandwich. Heat a non-stick or heavily seasoned skillet over medium heat 2-3 minutes. Place the sandwich in the skillet (it should sizzle at once) and grill 3-4 minutes until rich golden brown. Turn the sandwich carefully with a wide metal spatula, and grill the remaining side. Serve at once, hot from the skillet, with cranberry relish on the side.

SAUERKRAUT CHOUCROUTE WITH PARSLEYED POTATOES

Choucroute, a specialty of the Alsace area of France, is a Germanic-French favourite. Fresh sauerkraut, pungent with juniper berries, garlic, and onions, is slow-braised with smoked pork chops, assorted sausages, ham hocks, and slab bacon. This fabulous dish is brought to the table and served with parsleyed potatoes, crocks of assorted mustards, and good crusty bread. This is a great family and friends dish, to be shared by many. One helpful hint: don't use an aluminum pot for this recipe. The sauerkraut is quite acidic and may discolour. Serves 8-10.

6 tbsp.	vegetable oil or bacon drippings	90 mL
2	onions, chopped	2
3	large cloves garlic, minced	3
1 tbsp.	brown sugar	15 mL
2 tbsp.	*each* juniper berries and whole black peppercorns	30 mL
1 tbsp.	whole cloves	15 mL
2 cups	*each* dry white wine and apple cider	500 mL
4	bay leaves	4
4	smoked ham hocks, cracked	4
2 quarts	wine sauerkraut, rinsed and drained	2 L
2	6 oz. (180 g) pieces slab bacon, scored on top at 2 inch (5 cm) intervals	2
8-10	smoked pork chops, 1/2 inch (1 cm) thick	8-10
8-10	deli-style frankfurters (from the deli department)	8-10
8-10	smoked knockwurst	8-10
8-10	large boiling potatoes (red or white skinned), halved and soaked in cold water to cover	8-10
	butter	
	minced fresh parsley	
	salt and pepper to taste	
	Dijon, honey, and grainy mustards to taste	

In a very deep, heavy Dutch oven heat the vegetable oil over medium-high heat. Add the onions and sauté until translucent. Add the garlic and brown sugar, and sauté until golden brown. Stir in the juniper berries, peppercorns, cloves, white wine and cider, and bay leaves. Bring the mixture to a simmer and add the ham hocks, burying them into the sauerkraut to cover. Place the scored bacon slabs on top, cover the pot completely tight to seal, and simmer over low heat 3-4 hours or braise in a slow 300°F (150°C) oven.

Uncover the choucroute and add the smoked pork chops, frankfurters, and knockwurst. Partially cover and simmer 30 minutes. Let the finished dish rest 30 minutes while boiling the potatoes.

Cook the potatoes in simmering salted water until just fork-tender. Drain completely dry, toss with melted butter, and sprinkle with minced fresh parsley. Season with salt and pepper. Serve hot.

To present the choucroute: each serving should have a mound of the sauerkraut, a slice of the bacon, a serving of the ham hock, and 1 each pork chop, frankfurter, and knockwurst. Accompany each serving with 1 potato, and pass Dijon, grainy, and honey mustards as accompaniments.

The Easy Gourmet features a photograph of this recipe on page 17.

HOMEMADE SAUSAGE PATTIES WITH GLAZED APPLE RINGS

Tart, sweet apple rings add the perfect touch to this casual but delectable main course. Try it for a special brunch with scrambled eggs and juicy wedges of ripe tomato, or serve it with warmed dinner rolls and crunchy raw vegetables for a hearty family supper. You can make the patties ahead and pop them in the oven 15 minutes before serving time. Makes twelve 2 1/2 inch (6 cm) patties.

1 1/2 lbs.	boneless pork shoulder	750 g
1/2 lb.	thick cut bacon	250 g
4	slices dry firm white bread, coarsely crumbed (about 2 cups (500 mL))	4
1 - 1 1/2 tsp.	salt	5-7 mL
1 - 1 1/2 tsp.	ground sage	5-7 mL
1/2 tsp.	freshly ground black pepper	2 mL

Cut the pork and bacon into 1/2 inch (1 cm) cubes. Combine them in a large bowl and toss to mix, then process in the food processor until coarsely ground.

Place the bread crumbs in cold water until soaked through and squeeze them dry. Combine with the ground meat mixture. Add 1 tsp. (5 mL) each of the salt and sage and a dash of the pepper. Mix lightly but thoroughly. To taste for flavourings, do not eat the raw mixture but fry a small portion, cook and taste it. Adjust the seasonings.

Shape the sausage mixture into 12 patties, moistening your hands for easier handling. Arrange the patties in a single layer on a plate. Cover and refrigerate 24-48 hours to allow the flavours to mellow. Place the patties on a rack on a foil-lined baking sheet and bake at 350°F (180°C) until brown and crispy-looking, about 30 minutes. They may also be fried in a skillet over medium heat for about 15 minutes on each side or until cooked through.

Reheat them on a baking sheet at 350°F (180°C) for 15 minutes or until hot.

GLAZED APPLE RINGS

3-4	Granny Smith apples	3-4
	sugar to taste	
	butter to taste	

Peel, core, and thickly slice the apples. Dip them in sugar. Melt the butter in a skillet and gently fry the sugared rings. When they are golden on one side, turn and cook the other side. Place the rings on a lightly oiled plate to prevent sticking. Reheat in the oven at serving time.

OLD WORLD STUFFED CABBAGE ROLLS

These savoury lamb and rice-filled Middle Eastern cabbage rolls are braised with a piquant tomato-lemon sauce. Serve with rice or cracked wheat pilaf, and top with the pan juices. Serves 6-8.

2	large loose heads green cabbage	2
4 tbsp.	olive oil	60 mL
3 cups	diced onion	750 mL
2	cloves garlic, crushed	2
1 1/2 lbs.	lean ground lamb	750 g
1 tsp.	*each* salt and black pepper	5 mL
1/2 tsp.	ground cinnamon	2 mL
1/4 tsp.	ground allspice	1 mL
3 tbsp.	tomato paste	45 mL
1/2 cup	*each* uncooked white long-grain rice and water	125 mL
1/4 cup	*each* minced fresh parsley and mint	60 mL
1/3 cup	toasted pine nuts	75 mL
1 1/2 cups	tomato sauce	375 mL
1/3 cup	*each* fresh lemon juice and water	75 mL
3-4 tbsp.	chilled butter	45-60 mL
2 cups	plain yogurt, stirred smooth (optional)	500 mL

Remove the large outer leaves from the cabbage without tearing. Cut the largest leaves in half and blanch 2-3 minutes in boiling salted water until just tender. Drain on a clean towel, and set aside while preparing the filling.

Heat the olive oil in a large, deep skillet over medium-high heat. Add the onions and garlic, and sauté until softened. Increase the heat to high and brown the lamb, breaking it up with a fork. Season with the salt, pepper, cinnamon, allspice, and tomato paste. Heat until bubbly. Stir in the rice and water, and simmer, partially covered, until the rice is almost tender, about 8 minutes. Remove from heat. Stir in the minced parsley, mint, and pine nuts. Cool to room temperature.

Heat the oven to 350°F (180°C). Oil a heavy Dutch oven with a tight-fitting lid. Place 1 heaping tbsp. (15 mL) filling at one end of each leaf, tuck in the sides and roll into a sausage shape. Place the rolls seam side down in the pan in two layers. Combine the tomato sauce, lemon juice, and water. Pour evenly over cabbage rolls. Dot with cold butter. Cover tightly and bake 1 1/2 hours in the centre of the oven. Remove, uncover, and allow to rest

20-30 minutes before serving. Serve the rolls warm, each drizzled with some of the pan juices and topped with a dollop of cool yogurt, if desired.

SPICY LEMON AND ORANGE GLAZED LAMB SHANKS

Serve this meaty, succulent lamb entrée with cooked orzo (rice-shaped pasta), steamed fresh broccoli, and hot sourdough bread for dipping into the delicious sauce. Serves 4.

4 tbsp.	all-purpose flour	60 mL
1 tsp.	*each* salt, pepper, dried thyme, cinnamon, and paprika	5 mL
4	meaty lamb shanks, at room temperature	4
3 tbsp.	olive oil	45 mL
2	cloves garlic, slivered	2
1	medium onion, cut into thin slivers	1
1	*each* lemon and orange, cut into thin wedges	1
1	14 oz. (398 mL) can stewed tomatoes	1
1 tbsp.	sugar	15 mL
2	whole cinnamon sticks, 2 inches (5 cm) long	2
1/2 cup	black kalamata olives	125 mL
4 tbsp.	finely minced fresh parsley	60 mL

Combine the flour, salt, pepper, thyme, cinnamon, and paprika in a brown paper bag. Lightly dredge the lamb in the flour mixture.

Heat the olive oil in a large, wide Dutch oven. Sauté the garlic and onion 5 minutes, just until soft. Remove the vegetables with a slotted spoon, and set aside. Add the lamb to the hot oil. Brown quickly on all sides (do not pierce).

Add the lemon and orange to the pan, along with the tomatoes, sugar, sautéed garlic, and onion. Bring to a simmer, add the cinnamon sticks, and cover the pot. Simmer 2-2 1/2 hours, or until very tender. Baste frequently.

Lift the shanks and vegetables from the pot with a slotted spoon and place them on a warmed platter. Reduce the pan juices over high heat 3-5 minutes, until glossy and syrupy, adding the olives during the final 2 minutes. Pour the sauce over the shanks, sprinkle with minced parsley, and serve.

CHICKEN GOULASH WITH HERBED DUMPLINGS

Hungarian cuisine is renowned for its satisfying, spicy dishes, among them the famous goulash. Usually it is made with beef but this hearty variation, with its robust taste and wonderfully fragrant aroma, uses chicken. A deep dish is best for baking—it gives the fluffy dumplings lots of room to rise. Serve over rice and toss a bright green salad alongside. Serves 4.

1	2 1/2-3 lb. (1.25-1.5 kg) roasting chicken, jointed, or 1 1/2 lbs. (750 g) boneless chicken breasts, cut in small serving-size pieces	1
3 tbsp.	all-purpose flour	45 mL
1/4 tsp.	salt	1 mL
2 tbsp.	margarine or butter	30 mL
1 tbsp.	vegetable oil	15 mL
1	large onion, finely chopped	1
1 1/2 tbsp.	paprika	20 mL
1 1/2 cups	chicken stock	375 mL
3	large tomatoes, cored, seeded, and chopped	3
1	medium green bell pepper, sliced	1
2 tbsp.	tomato paste	30 mL
1 tsp.	sugar	5 mL
1/2 tsp.	dried marjoram	2 mL
1	bay leaf	1
pinch	ground nutmeg	pinch
	Herbed Dumplings (recipe follows)	
2/3 cup	sour cream	150 mL

Place the chicken pieces in a large bowl. Sprinkle on the flour and salt and toss to coat well. In a large, deep saucepan, heat the margarine and oil. Add the chicken and any loose flour and sauté over medium-high heat until golden on all sides, turning occasionally. Remove from the pan and set aside.

Add the onion to the pan and sauté over medium heat for 2-3 minutes until soft, scraping the bottom of the pan. Stir in the paprika and sauté for 30 seconds. Pour in the stock, stirring. Add the tomatoes, pepper, tomato paste, sugar, marjoram, bay leaf, and nutmeg. Bring to a boil, stirring. Return the chicken to the pan, cover, and simmer about 40 minutes, or until the chicken is tender.

Heat the oven to 350°F (180°C). A few minutes before the chicken is cooked, prepare the dumplings.

HERBED DUMPLINGS

1 cup	all-purpose flour	250 mL
1 1/2 tsp.	baking powder	7 mL
1/4 tsp.	salt	1 mL
3 tbsp.	margarine	45 mL
2 tbsp.	chopped fresh parsley	30 mL
3 tbsp.	water	45 mL

In a medium bowl, mix the flour, baking powder, and salt. Add the margarine and cut it into the flour until the mixture resembles fine bread crumbs. Stir in the parsley. Pour in the water and mix to a soft dough. Divide the mixture into 8 portions and form each piece into a ball.

Remove the chicken and sauce from the pan and place in a deep 10 cup (2.5 L) casserole dish. Arrange the dumplings around the outer edge, on top of the chicken. Cover and bake 20-25 minutes, until the dumplings are well risen and cooked.

Spoon the sour cream into the middle of the casserole and serve.

TARRAGON-SOUR CREAM CHICKEN

The flavours of classic French cooking blend together in this recipe, simple enough for a busy weekday dinner and elegant enough for guests. Serve it with fluffy microwave-cooked rice and a salad of butter lettuce and oranges tossed in an orange juice and tarragon vinegar dressing. Serves 3-4.

3-3 1/2 lbs.	chicken pieces	1.5-1.75 kg
1	medium onion, chopped	1
2 tbsp.	butter	30 mL
3 tbsp.	all-purpose flour	45 mL
1/2 tsp.	*each* salt and black pepper	2 mL
2 cups	chicken stock or broth	500 mL
1	bay leaf	1
3 tbsp.	chopped fresh tarragon	45 mL
1 cup	sour cream	250 mL

Place the chicken pieces in a single layer in a shallow microproof dish, arranging the thicker parts towards the outside edge.

Place the onion and butter in a 4 cup (1 L) microproof measure. Cover and microwave on HIGH 100% power 2-3 minutes until the onion is soft. Blend in the flour, salt, and pepper. Gradually blend in the stock. Microwave on HIGH 100% power in 2 minute increments until the sauce comes to a boil and thickens, stirring well after each cooking period. Stir in the bay leaf and tarragon. Pour the sauce over the chicken pieces, cover with waxed paper and microwave on MEDIUM HIGH 70% power, allowing 6-8 minutes per pound. Rearrange the chicken pieces halfway through the cooking time.

Place the sour cream in the measure. Drain the sauce from the cooked chicken into the measure and blend with the sour cream. Pour the sour cream sauce over the chicken, cover with waxed paper and microwave on MEDIUM 50% power 3-5 minutes until the sauce is heated through.

To serve, discard the bay leaf, arrange the chicken on a serving platter and top with the sauce.

Opposite: (top to bottom) Mexican Olive-Raisin Meat Loaf (p. 16), Double-Olive Mediterranean Beef Stew (p. 86).

RANGE BAKED CHICKEN

Thin slices of orange form a beautiful—and deliciously juicy—pattern under the skin of a tender roasting chicken in this company recipe. Roasted in a "self-basting" bag for succulent meat and a ready-made sauce, the chicken almost takes care of itself. Julienned vegetables such as carrot, turnips, and beans make a nice accompaniment. Serves 4.

1	4 1/2 lb. (2.25 kg) roasting chicken	1
2	navel oranges, thinly sliced	2
1 tbsp.	oil	15 mL
1 tbsp.	*each* salt, paprika, and pepper	15 mL
1	small onion, quartered	1
1 tbsp.	all-purpose flour	15 mL
1/2 cup	frozen orange juice concentrate, thawed	125 mL

Heat the oven to 325°F (160°C). Dry the chicken with paper towels.

Place the chicken on a work surface, breast side up. Starting above the cavity, carefully separate the skin from the flesh with your hands. Work around the breast, towards the wings and down around the leg, being careful not to tear the skin. Tuck the orange slices under the skin in an overlapping pattern. Rub the chicken well with oil. Mix the salt, paprika, and pepper together and season the chicken inside and out, rubbing the mixture into the skin. Place the onion and any leftover oranges in the cavity. Truss the chicken by tying the legs and wings close to the body.

Place the flour in a large self-basting bag with the chicken. Shake well to coat the chicken with flour. Add the orange juice concentrate. Tie the bag and place it on a baking sheet. (The dish may be made ahead to this point and refrigerated.)

To bake, snip the self-basting bag in several places and place it in the oven. Roast until the chicken registers 160°F (70°C) on an instant thermometer or is dark golden brown and a leg moves easily, about 2 1/2 hours.

Remove the chicken from the oven and carefully open the bag, transferring the juices to a saucepan. Skim off as much fat as possible. Boil the sauce until reduced to 1 cup (250 mL). Taste and correct for seasonings.

Carve the chicken into serving pieces and serve the sauce alongside.

NEW WAVE CHICKEN AND DUMPLINGS

On a cold wintery night, nothing is more inviting than a warming supper of tender chicken and fluffy dumplings. Serve with a fresh green salad, steamed whole baby carrots, and glasses of cold milk. Serves 6-8.

1	3 1/2 lb. (1.75 kg) frying chicken, cut up	1
4 tbsp.	butter	60 mL
3	thick slices bacon, coarsely chopped	3
1	medium onion, coarsely chopped	1
1/2 lb.	fresh small mushrooms, wiped clean with a damp cloth (do not wash)	250 g
6 tbsp.	all-purpose flour	90 mL
2 cups	chicken stock	500 mL
1/2 cup	dry sherry or apple cider	125 mL
1 tsp.	*each* salt and dry mustard	5 mL
1/2 tsp.	black pepper	2 mL
1 cup	*each* milk and cream	250 mL
	Dumplings (recipe follows)	

Rinse the chicken pieces in cool water and pat them completely dry. Heat the butter in a 6 quart (6 L) heavy pan over medium-high heat. Add the chicken pieces and brown quickly, turning, until the chicken is pale golden on all sides. Remove the chicken to a platter, and set it aside. Into the remaining drippings, stir the chopped bacon and onion. Sauté, stirring, until softened and pale golden. Remove the mixture with a slotted spoon, leaving the drippings in the pan, and add to the chicken. Add the mushrooms to the pan and quickly sauté over medium-high heat, stirring, to brown on all sides (if the mushrooms are cooked over lower heat, they will "sweat" and become soggy). Remove the mushrooms with a slotted spoon, add them to the chicken and set the chicken mixture aside.

Sprinkle the flour over the remaining drippings in the pan, loosen up any bits clinging to the bottom of the pan, and cook until bubbly, about 3 minutes. Whisk in the chicken stock, sherry, salt, mustard, and pepper, and bring to a boil. Add the milk and cream, whisking until smooth. Taste and correct the seasonings.

Add the chicken and the reserved vegetables to the pan. Bring the mixture to a simmer over low heat, partially cover, and cook 30 minutes, until the chicken is almost tender. Skim off and discard any fat that rises to the surface.

DUMPLINGS

2 cups	all-purpose flour	500 mL
4 tsp.	baking powder	20 mL
1/2 tsp.	*each* salt and pepper	2 mL
1 tbsp.	*each* minced fresh parsley, chives, tarragon, and dill	15 mL
1 tbsp.	finely grated lemon rind	15 mL
6 tbsp.	chilled butter	90 mL
1 cup	buttermilk	250 mL

Sift together the flour, baking powder, salt, and pepper. Whisk in the minced fresh parsley, chives, tarragon, dill, and lemon rind. With a pastry blender, cut in the butter until the mixture resembles coarse crumbs. Add the buttermilk and stir lightly with a fork until the dough holds together and cleans the sides of the bowl.

Gently form the dough into 6 large or 12 small balls, handling them lightly. Drop the dumpling mixture over the top of the chicken mixture in large dessert-spoonfuls, leaving a bit of space between them for expansion. Cover the pot completely with a domed lid and cook over low heat about 20-25 minutes until the dumplings are risen and firm to the touch (don't peek!). The dumplings are done when a toothpick inserted in the centre comes out clean.

Serve at once, piping hot, ladled into wide shallow soup bowls with the dumplings on top.

CHICKEN BREASTS WITH MUSTARD CREAM SAUCE

This delicious dish is hearty enough for a family meal and elegant enough for entertaining. Succulent chicken breasts are done to a quick, golden turn in a skillet, and finished with a pan sauce of shallots, mustard and cream. Serve with crispy ultra-thin shoestring potatoes, fresh green beans, a leafy bibb lettuce salad, and warm dinner rolls. Serves 4.

1/2 cup	flour	125 mL
1/2 tsp.	*each* salt, pepper, and ground nutmeg	2 mL
4	whole boneless chicken breasts, skin attached	4
4 tbsp.	butter	60 mL
1/3 cup	shallots, finely minced	75 mL
2 tbsp.	*each* fresh lemon juice and dry vermouth	30 mL
1 cup	whipping cream	250 mL
2 tbsp.	ice cold butter	30 mL
	salt and pepper to taste	
2 tbsp.	Dijon mustard	30 mL
2 tbsp.	finely minced fresh parsley	30 mL

Whisk together the flour, salt, pepper, and nutmeg. Lightly dredge each chicken breast in the mixture and shake off the excess. Place the floured breasts on a wire rack for 30 minutes to "air dry."

In a large non-stick skillet, heat the 4 tbsp. (60 mL) butter over medium heat until bubbly. Add the chicken breasts, skin side down, and sauté 7-8 minutes or until rich golden brown. Shake the pan frequently to keep the skin from sticking. Using tongs, turn each breast and sauté 7-8 minutes longer, or until golden brown. When pressed, the chicken should feel just firmed and slightly resilient. Remove the breasts from the pan, and place on a warm platter.

Discard all but 2 tbsp. (30 mL) of the drippings. Increase the heat to medium-high, and sauté the shallots until translucent and pale golden, 2-3 minutes. Add the lemon juice and vermouth, and deglaze the pan (stir up any juices and drippings left clinging to it) over high heat until the glaze is syrupy, bubbly, and clear. Add the cream, whisk smooth, and reduce to about one-half over high heat. The sauce should be bubbly and should coat a spoon nicely.

Remove the skillet from the heat and swirl in the cold butter in several pieces, one at a time, to enrich the sauce. Add salt and pepper to taste. Swirl in the mustard, whisk smooth, and spoon the hot sauce over the chicken so it is partially covered. Sprinkle lightly with minced parsley and serve at once.

Note: To the finished sauce, you may stir in 2 tbsp. (30 mL) drained green peppercorns, and 1-2 tbsp. (15-30 mL) finely minced fresh tarragon or chives.

GAME HENS WITH APPLES AND MUSTARD CREAM SAUCE

Moist, flavourful, and lovely to present, game hens make a wonderful dish for entertaining. The tender meat works beautifully cooked slowly in the oven with its creamy, rich sauce. Serve it with Mustard Scalloped Potatoes (p. 77) and a steamed bright green vegetable. Serves 4.

2	game hens, about 1 1/4 lb. (625 g) each	2
3 tbsp.	margarine or butter	45 mL
1 tbsp.	vegetable oil	15 mL
2	medium Golden Delicious apples	2
1	medium onion, chopped	1
2 tbsp.	all-purpose flour	30 mL
1 1/2 cups	chicken stock	375 mL
pinch	dried mixed herbs	pinch
1/2 tbsp.	Dijon mustard	7 mL
1/3 cup	whipping cream	75 mL
1 tbsp.	chopped fresh chives or parsley	15 mL
	salt and pepper to taste	

Heat the oven to 350°F (180°C). Split each game hen in half, cutting lengthwise through the centre backbone. In a large skillet, melt 2 tbsp. (30 mL) of the margarine with the oil. Sauté the game hens over medium heat, turning to brown on all sides, about 10 minutes. Place the hens in a casserole dish large enough to hold them in a single layer. Peel, core, and slice one of the apples. Place it in the skillet with the onion and sauté over medium heat 4 minutes. Stir in the flour and cook, stirring, for 1 minute. Pour in the stock gradually and bring to a boil, stirring. Add the mixed herbs and pour the sauce over the game hens. Cover and bake for 1 hour, until tender.

Remove the game hens from the casserole and strain the sauce into a small saucepan, pressing well with a wooden spoon to push all the juices through. Return the hens to the casserole dish and keep warm. Cook the sauce over medium to medium-high heat until it is reduced to 1 cup (250 mL), about 20 minutes. Reduce the heat to low and stir in the mustard, cream, and chives. Season to taste with salt and pepper. Set aside.

In a small skillet, melt the remaining 1 tbsp. (15 mL) margarine. Peel, core and slice the remaining apple and sauté it in the skillet, turning, until golden brown. Gently heat the sauce through, pour it over the hens, sprinkle on the fried apples, and serve.

ORANGE ROUGHY WITH GINGER AND PINEAPPLE

Firm, tasty fish coated with a sprightly, Oriental-inspired sauce, this dish is simply wonderful with New Zealand orange roughy, a white fish with a texture like halibut, but try the recipe with any firm-textured white fish. Serve it with a generous mound of brown rice and a colourful mixture of steamed fresh vegetables. Serves 4.

4	medium orange roughy fillets, thawed	4
2 tbsp.	lemon juice	30 mL
1/2 cup	water	125 mL
1 tbsp.	apple juice or sherry	15 mL
2 tsp.	grated fresh ginger	10 mL
3 tbsp.	cornstarch	45 mL
1 tbsp.	sugar	15 mL
1	pineapple slice, diced (optional)	1
	a few gratings of carrot for garnish	

Heat the oven to 400°F (200°C). Grease an 8 x 8 inch (20 x 20 cm) baking dish. Place the fish in the prepared dish.

Put the lemon juice, water, apple juice, and ginger in a medium saucepan. In a small bowl, stir together the cornstarch and sugar. Add a little of the lemon mixture to the cornstarch mixture to make a smooth paste, then add it all to the saucepan and bring it to a slow boil, stirring constantly. Cook for 1 minute. Stir in the pineapple. Pour the sauce over the fish fillets.

Bake 25-30 minutes, until the fish is opaque and flakes easily with a fork. About 10 minutes before the fish is done, add the carrot garnish.

SALMON FISH CAKES WITH BURNT CHIVE BUTTER

Salmon fish cakes turn cupboard ingredients into a nutritious, melt-in-your-mouth family supper. Make them up ahead of time, then quickly fry them just before serving. A dish of Burnt Chive Butter and a colourful selection of steamed fresh vegetables are all you need to complete the meal. Serves 6.

1 1/2 lbs.	potatoes, peeled and chopped	750 g
2	7 1/2 oz. (213 g) cans sockeye salmon, drained and flaked	2
4 tbsp.	chopped fresh parsley	60 mL
1/2 tsp.	salt	2 mL
1/4 tsp.	pepper	1 mL
3	eggs	3
	all-purpose flour	
1 1/4 cups	fine French bread crumbs	300 mL
	vegetable oil, for frying	
	Burnt Chive Butter (recipe follows)	

In a saucepan, cook the potatoes in boiling water about 15 minutes, until cooked. Drain well and mash. Return to a low heat and stir constantly 1 minute to dry the potatoes. Remove them from the heat.

Stir in the salmon, parsley, salt, and pepper. Beat 1 of the eggs and stir it into the potato mixture. (The mixture should not be too soft.) Divide the mixture into 12 equal portions, about 1/3 cup (75 mL) each. On a floured surface, use a spatula to shape each portion into a round flat cake about 2 1/2 inches (6 cm) across and 1/2 inch (1 cm) thick. Roll all sides lightly in flour.

Beat the remaining eggs in a shallow bowl and spread the bread crumbs on a large plate. Brush each fish cake first with egg, then coat it all over with bread crumbs. Re-shape the cakes. Place them on a flat platter, cover with plastic wrap and refrigerate 1 hour so the mixture can firm up.

Into a large skillet, pour just enough oil to cover the bottom and fry the fish cakes a few at a time, over medium heat, about 8 minutes or until golden brown on both sides. Turn the heat to low if they brown too quickly. Drain on paper towelling and keep warm.

BURNT CHIVE BUTTER

1/3 cup	butter	75 mL
1 tsp.	lemon juice	5 mL
2 tbsp.	chopped fresh chives	30 mL

In a small, heavy-based pan, melt the butter over medium heat. Turn the heat to high and cook the butter until it just starts to turn brown, watching it constantly. Immediately remove it from the heat, pour in the lemon juice, and add the chives. Serve hot with the fish cakes.

GREEK-STYLE SKILLET PRAWNS WITH FETA

Healthy, zesty with flavour, vibrant with colour, fun to eat—no wonder Greek food is so wildly popular, and this unique recipe for prawns baked with feta is one more reason to love it! Serve with hot grilled pita breads, orzo (rice-shaped pasta) or rice pilaf, and a big salad of cucumbers and tomatoes dressed with olive oil, lemon juice, and Greek olives. Serves 4.

1/2 cup	olive oil	125 mL
1	medium onion, halved and thinly sliced	1
1	bunch green onions, trimmed and thinly sliced	1
3	cloves garlic, slivered	3
2 1/2 cups	firm fresh tomatoes or Roma tomatoes, peeled and coarsely chopped	625 mL
1 tsp.	sugar	5 mL
1/2 cup	dry white wine or vermouth	125 mL
4 tbsp.	minced fresh parsley	60 mL
1 1/2 tsp.	dried oregano, crumbled	7 mL
	salt and freshly ground black pepper to taste	
1 1/2 lbs.	very large prawns, deveined and shelled, tails intact	750 kg
8 oz.	feta cheese, drained and very coarsely crumbled	250 g
	lemon wedges	

Heat the olive oil in a large skillet over medium-high heat until it sizzles. Add the onions and green onions and sauté, stirring, until translucent and pale golden. Add the garlic and sauté 2 minutes. Increase the heat to high, add the tomatoes and sugar, and cook until the tomatoes release and re-absorb their juices. Stir in the white wine, parsley, oregano, salt, and liberal grindings black pepper. Partially cover the skillet and simmer 25 minutes. The sauce should be quite thick. Heat the oven to 400°F (200°C).

Liberally brush an ovenproof oval baking dish with olive oil. Transfer the mixture to the dish. Tuck the prawns into the sauce, tails out, and sprinkle the top with crumbled feta. Bake in the centre of the oven about 10-12 minutes, just until the prawns are cooked and the feta has melted. Serve at once over hot orzo or rice. Garnish each portion with lemon wedges.

ID-WEST PEROGIES WITH SPICED ONIONS

Perogies are such a comforting, homey, satisfying dish—just the thing to sit down to when the weather turns a bit cold and damp. The freezer section boasts a wide variety of tempting perogies, ready to pop into boiling water at a moment's notice. Filled with potato, cheese, sauerkraut, or cottage cheese, and all wrapped up in a smooth "envelope," perogies are simply delicious fare. Serve with hot grilled Ukrainian sausage from the deli meats section and a leafy green salad, and you have a hearty feast indeed! Serves 4.

1 tbsp.	*each* salt and vegetable oil	15 mL
4 tbsp.	vegetable oil	60 mL
2 tbsp.	butter or bacon drippings	30 mL
2	very large onions (about 1 lb. (500 g)), thinly sliced	2
1 tbsp.	brown sugar	15 mL
	salt and cracked black pepper to taste	
1/4 tsp.	*each* ground coriander, allspice, and nutmeg	1 mL
1 tsp.	paprika	5 mL
	several large dashes bottled hot pepper sauce	
2 tsp.	cider vinegar	10 mL
1	1 lb. 5 oz. (500 g) pkg. frozen perogies, any filling	1
1 cup	sour cream	250 mL

Bring several quarts water to a boil in a large stock pot, adding the 1 tbsp. (15 mL) each salt and vegetable oil to the water. While the water is coming to a boil, heat a very large non-stick skillet and add the oil and butter. Heat over medium-high heat until sizzling. Add the sliced onions, and toss quickly to coat with oil. Fry the onion, tossing with a wooden spoon, 8-10 minutes until crispy and golden brown. Add the sugar after 5 minutes (sugar will help the onions to carmelize). Sprinkle on the salt, pepper, coriander, allspice, nutmeg, and paprika. Fry the onions 3-4 minutes longer. Add the hot pepper sauce and cider vinegar, increase the heat to high, and cook 2-3 minutes until glazed and crisp. Set onions aside.

Following the package directions, drop the frozen perogies into boiling water. After they float to the top, cook 5 minutes or until tender. Remove with a slotted spoon to a warmed bowl or platter, top with the hot fried onions and serve at once on warmed crockery plates, adding a generous dollop of sour cream to each portion.

Note: Follow package directions for pan-fried perogies if desired and serve with the spiced fried onions and sour cream.

CASSEROLES

Versatile, tasty, and convenient, casseroles are family favourites. The recipes in this section are specially designed to double as company dishes, so whatever the occasion, try Spiced Beef and Walnut Pie or Turkey Ratatouille or Red Snapper Mexicana—good, tasty fare that comes to the table in one warm, fragrant dish.

CASSOULET OF SAUSAGE AND BEANS

This recipe, made famous in southwestern France, calls for lots of ingredients, but it is easy, full-flavoured, and loaded with fibre and protein. Serves 8.

Bean Mixture

2	14 oz. (398 mL) cans beans with pork	2
1	14 oz. (398 mL) can kidney beans, undrained	1
1	14 oz. (398 mL) can green or yellow lima beans, undrained	1
2 tbsp.	brown sugar	30 mL
1/2 tsp.	dry mustard	2 mL
1/4 tsp.	salt	1 mL
dash	freshly ground black pepper	dash

Meat Mixture

3/4 - 1 lb.	ground beef	375-500 g
1 lb.	smoked sausage (try salami or beer), cut into 1/2 inch (1 cm) cubes	500 g
2	small onions, sliced into rings	2
	salt and pepper to taste	

Sauce

1/2 cup	ketchup	125 mL
4 tbsp.	water	60 mL
1 tbsp.	vinegar	15 mL
1 tsp.	sugar	5 mL
1/4 tsp.	dry mustard	1 mL

Heat the oven to 350°F (180°C). Grease a 2 1/2-3 quart (2.5-3 L) ovenproof casserole. In it, mix together the ingredients for the bean mixture. Bake 30 minutes. Shape the ground beef into 1 inch (2.5 cm) balls. Cook in a skillet over medium heat until lightly browned. Add the sausage, onions, and seasonings. Cook until the onions are tender and the meat is no longer pink. Combine the sauce ingredients and pour over the meat. Cover and simmer 10 minutes. Add the simmered meat and sauce mixture to the beans. Bake until bubbly, about 15-20 minutes. Serve hot.

BEEF CASSEROLE DELUXE

Here is a tasty way to use up leftover roast—a hot, nutrition-packed casserole with a tangy, crispy topping. All it needs is a tossed green salad and a medley of fresh steamed vegetables. Serves 4.

2 cups	broad egg noodles	500 mL
2 cups	cubed cooked roast beef	500 mL
2 cups	sliced mushrooms	500 mL
1	medium onion, chopped	1
1 tbsp.	butter	15 mL
1	large carrot, chopped	1
1 cup	low-fat cottage cheese	250 mL
1/2 cup	beef juice, leftover gravy, or broth	125 mL
1/2 cup + 1 tbsp.	chopped fresh parsley	140 mL
1 tbsp.	Worcestershire sauce	15 mL
	salt and pepper to taste	
1 tsp.	curry powder (optional)	5 mL
2 tbsp.	fine dry bread crumbs	30 mL
2 tbsp.	grated Parmesan cheese	30 mL

Grease an 8 inch (20 cm) square pan. Boil the noodles in a large pot of water until tender. Drain and spread in the pan. Top with the beef. Sauté the mushrooms and onion in the butter until tender. Spoon the mixture over the beef. Cook the carrot until tender and purée thoroughly with the cottage cheese. Stir in the beef juice and 1/2 cup (125 mL) of the parsley. Season with Worcestershire, salt, pepper, and curry. Spoon this mixture over the casserole, pushing it into the mushrooms and beef.

Heat the oven to 350°F (180°C). Mix together the bread crumbs, Parmesan, and the remaining 1 tbsp. (15 mL) parsley and sprinkle over top. Bake 45-60 minutes or until bubbling and heated through.

SPICED BEEF AND WALNUT PIE

Meat pies are a family favourite, and this one is good enough for company too. Meaty chunks of stew beef are simmered to tender perfection, then topped with freshly baked walnut-studded scones. Add a salad of curly greens and you have a filling, nutritious, tasty dinner. Serves 4-6.

1 1/2 lbs.	stew beef, trimmed and cut into 1 inch (2.5 cm) cubes	750 g
4 tbsp.	all-purpose flour	60 mL
1 tsp.	*each* paprika and curry powder	5 mL
1/4 tsp.	*each* salt and pepper	1 mL
3 tbsp.	margarine or butter	45 mL
2	medium onions, thinly sliced	2
1 1/4 cups	beef stock	300 mL
1 tsp.	*each* vinegar and brown sugar	5 mL
1/2 tsp.	Worcestershire sauce	2 mL
1/4 tsp.	ground nutmeg	1 mL
1/2 cup	toasted walnuts	125 mL

WALNUT-HERB SCONES

2 cups	all-purpose flour	500 mL
4 tsp.	baking powder	20 mL
1/4 tsp.	salt	1 mL
1/2 cup	vegetable shortening	125 mL
4 tbsp.	chopped fresh parsley or chives	60 mL
1/3 cup	finely chopped walnuts	75 mL
2/3 cup	milk	150 mL

Heat the oven to 350°F (180°C).

Place the meat in a large bowl. Add the flour, paprika, curry, salt, and pepper. Toss to coat well.

In a large saucepan, melt the margarine. Add the meat and onions and sauté, stirring, over medium-high heat, about 4 minutes or until the meat loses its pink colour. Pour in the stock and stir in the vinegar, brown sugar,

Worcestershire sauce, and nutmeg. Pour the mixture into a 10 cup (2.5 L) oval casserole dish. Cover and bake for 1 3/4-2 hours, or until the meat is tender. Remove the meat from the oven and stir in the walnuts. Set aside while you make the scones.

Increase the oven temperature to 425°F (220°C). Place the flour, baking powder, and salt in a medium bowl. Add the shortening and cut it into the flour until the mixture resembles fine bread crumbs. Stir in the parsley and walnuts. Pour in the milk and mix with a knife to make a soft dough. Form the dough into a round, being careful not to overhandle. Roll out on a lightly floured surface to 1/2 inch (1 cm) thickness. Cut out scones with a 2 1/2 inch (6 cm) fluted cutter (this recipe makes about 11 scones).

Arrange the scones on top of the meat, slightly overlapping, around the edge of the casserole dish. Bake, uncovered, 15-20 minutes or until the meat is heated through and the scones are risen and golden. Serve hot.

TARRAGON PORK PIE

In this flavour update on the classic meat pie, ground pork is spiced up with crisp bacon, chopped shallots, and a touch of tarragon, and it's all enclosed in a tender pastry crust. Save yourself some time by picking up a package of pastry from the freezer section. Baked potatoes and a tender-crisp stir-fry of fresh vegetables are great accompaniments. Serves 6.

6	slices bacon, chopped	6
2	shallots, finely chopped	2
1 lb.	ground pork	500 g
2 tbsp.	all-purpose flour	30 mL
2/3 cup	chicken stock	150 mL
4	green onions, chopped	4
1 tsp.	dried tarragon	5 mL
1/4 tsp.	*each* salt and pepper	1 mL
1	13 oz. (400 g) package frozen pie pastry, thawed	1
	beaten egg or milk for glaze	

In a medium saucepan, sauté the bacon until crisp. Add the shallots and sauté until soft but not brown, about 2 minutes. Add the pork and stir with a wooden spoon to break up the meat. Cook over medium-high heat for 5 minutes, stirring occasionally. Drain off all but 2 tbsp. (30 mL) of the fat. Stir in the flour and cook 1 minute, stirring. Pour in the stock and bring to a boil, stirring. Cover the pan and simmer over low heat 5 minutes. Remove from the heat, stir in the green onions, tarragon, salt, and pepper, and allow to cool.

Heat the oven to 400°F (200°C). Roll out just over half of the pastry and line the bottom of a deep 9 inch (23 cm) pie plate. Spoon in the cooled pork mixture. Roll out the remaining pastry for the lid. Dampen the pastry edges with water and cover the meat mixture with the pastry lid. Press the edges together to seal, trim and flute the edges. With a sharp knife, cut 2 slits in the top of the pastry for the steam to escape. Brush the lid with egg or milk and bake 15 minutes. Reduce the heat to 350°F (180°C) and bake 30-40 minutes longer, until the pie is golden brown.

The Easy Gourmet features a photograph of this recipe on page 53 (facing).

Opposite: (top to bottom) Shrimp-Crab-Mushroom Quiche (p. 67), Quebec Tourtière (p. 56), Tarragon Pork Pie (p. 52).

OLASSES BAKED BEANS WITH SPARERIBS

This meal-in-a-dish, perfect for the cold winter weather, needs only a basket of thick-sliced toasted whole grain bread and a spicy tomato salad to satisfy everyone at the dinner table. The beans freeze and reheat well—in fact, reheating enhances and develops the flavour. Serves 8-10.

6 cups	water	1.5 L
1	1 lb. (500 g) pkg. Great Northern beans	1
2 lbs.	country-style pork spareribs, cut into bite-size pieces	1 kg
1	large onion, chopped	1
4 tbsp.	blackstrap molasses	60 mL
1 tbsp.	Worcestershire sauce	15 mL
1 tsp.	dried mustard	5 mL
1 tsp.	ground ginger	5 mL
1/2 tsp.	garlic powder	2 mL
1 tbsp.	salt	15 mL
2 tsp.	freshly ground black pepper	10 mL
1	5.5 oz. (156 mL) can tomato paste	1

In a large microproof casserole, place the water, beans, spareribs, and onion. Cover and microwave on HIGH 100% power 20 minutes.

Stir in the remaining ingredients. Cover and microwave on MEDIUM 50% power 1 1/2 hours, stirring after each 30 minutes of cooking time. Reduce the power level to MEDIUM LOW 30% and microwave 30-50 minutes longer, until the beans are tender.

Taste and correct for salt and pepper.

Let stand, covered, for about 10 minutes before serving.

QUEBEC TOURTIÈRE

Tourtière has been a French Canadian Christmas tradition for years, and it's great in any winter dinner menu with just a leafy green salad on the side. Serves 6-8.

2	12 oz. (400 g) pkgs. frozen pie pastry, thawed	2
	Dijon mustard to taste	
2 tbsp.	vegetable oil	30 mL
2 cups	diced onion (1 large onion)	500 mL
2	cloves garlic, minced	2
1 tbsp.	sugar	15 mL
1 1/2 lbs.	lean ground pork	750 g
2 tsp.	*each* salt, freshly ground black pepper, and crumbled dried sage	10 mL
1 tsp.	*each* dry mustard, ground nutmeg, allspice, and coriander	5 mL
1/2 tsp.	*each* ground cinnamon and celery seed	2 mL
1/2 cup	water	125 mL
3 tbsp.	butter	45 mL
1/2 lb.	fresh mushrooms, sliced	250 g
1/2 lb.	ham trimmings, coarsely diced	250 g
1 1/2 cups	fresh bread crumbs	375 mL
1	egg	1
2 tbsp.	half-and-half cream	30 mL

Roll out one package of the thawed pastry on a lightly floured surface to 1/4 inch (6 mm) thick. Gather the dough up on a rolling pin and gently ease it into a 10 inch (25 cm) metal springform pan with 2 inch (5 cm) high sides, making sure not to stretch it. Cut the pastry to hang over the top edges 1 inch (2.5 cm) all around. Brush the bottom of the pastry with Dijon mustard and chill while preparing filling. Gather up and save any pastry scraps.

Heat the oil in a large skillet over medium-high heat. Add the onions and garlic and sauté, stirring, until softened and pale golden. Add the sugar and sauté 1-2 minutes longer. Stir in the meat and sauté until it is no longer pink. Add the salt, pepper, sage, dry mustard, nutmeg, allspice, coriander, cinnamon, and celery seed. Cook over high heat 3-4 minutes. The mixture should be glossy and pulpy-thick. Add the water and cook over high heat

5-7 minutes until syrupy. Remove the skillet from the heat and set aside.

In a small skillet, heat the butter over medium-high heat until bubbly. Quickly sauté the mushrooms until pale golden and dry. Combine the meat mixture, mushrooms, ham, and bread crumbs. Mix gently but thoroughly. Cool completely.

Spoon the cooled filling into the chilled pastry shell. Gently level the top. Roll out the remaining pastry into a 14 inch (35 cm) round. Drape the pastry over the pie. Moisten the edges with water and seal. Flute the border in a decorative manner, making sure the border stays on the inside edge of the pan. For an extra special touch, gather all pastry scraps, re-roll, and cut into decorative shapes. Moisten with water and arrange them on the top crust. Cut several deep V-shaped steam vents in the top.

Beat the egg with the cream. Brush the glaze evenly over the top of the pie. If desired, refrigerate, uncovered, 4-6 hours or overnight.

Heat the oven to 425°F (220°C). Bake the pie in the lower third of the oven for 15 minutes. Reduce the temperature to 350°F (180°C) and bake 60 minutes longer, or until the pastry is a deep, rich, golden brown. If the pie is browning too quickly, cover loosely with aluminum foil. The pie is done when the filling begins to bubble up through the steam vents. Remove it from the oven and cool on a wire rack 2-3 hours. Release the pie from the pan, slice, and serve warm or at room temperature, accompanied by Spiced Chunky Applesauce.

SPICED CHUNKY APPLESAUCE

1 cup	apple cider	250 mL
2 cups	sugar	500 mL
5 lbs.	golden delicious or Rome beauty apples, or a combination, peeled, cored,and cut into large chunks	2.5 kg
1 tbsp.	fresh lemon juice	15 mL
1-2 tsp.	finely grated lemon rind	5-10 mL
1/2 tsp.	*each* ground cinnamon, nutmeg, and ginger	2 mL
dash	ground allspice	dash

Combine the cider and sugar and cook over medium-high heat until the sugar dissolves. Add the apples, bring the mixture to a simmer, and cook 1 hour until the apples are very soft, almost dissolved. Stir in the lemon juice, rind, cinnamon, nutmeg, ginger, and allspice. Cook 1 hour longer over low heat. Cool completely, cap tightly, and chill until ready to serve.

The Easy Gourmet features a photograph of this recipe on page 53.

PRAIRIE-STYLE HAM AND SCALLOPED POTATOES

This is such a satisfying supper dish that it needs only a bowl of steaming, bright green broccoli, a crisp green salad, and a loaf of hot crusty bread to complete the meal. Old-fashioned and simple, this is good comfort food to come home to. Serves 6.

6	large russet potatoes, peeled and soaked in cold water to cover	6
6 tbsp.	butter	90 mL
2	large onions, halved and sliced	2
1 1/2 tsp.	sugar	7 mL
1 cup	fresh bread crumbs, air-dried 3-4 hours	250 mL
12 oz.	shaved smoked ham	375 g
8 oz.	imported Emmenthal (Swiss) or Gruyere cheese, coarsely grated	250 g
	freshly ground black pepper and ground nutmeg to taste	
2 cups	whipping cream, scalded and hot	500 mL
4 tbsp.	*each* fresh bread crumbs and Parmesan cheese	60 mL

Bring a large pot of water to a boil. Slice each potato into 1/2 inch (1 cm) thick rounds, and drop into the boiling water. Cook about 5 minutes or until just slightly tender. Drain completely dry on a clean towel.

Melt 4 tbsp. (60 mL) of the butter in a large skillet over medium-high heat. Sauté the onions until golden brown, adding the sugar after 3-4 minutes to carmelize the onions. Set aside. Fry the 1 cup (250 mL) bread crumbs in the remaining 2 tbsp. (30 mL) butter until golden. Set aside. Heat the oven to 375°F (190°C).

Lightly butter a large oval baking dish. Layer in half the onions, potatoes, ham shavings, cheese, and browned bread crumbs, seasoning with pepper and nutmeg. Repeat.

Cover the assembled dish with the hot scalded cream, pouring it over slowly and evenly. Allow the cream to settle 5 minutes. Sprinkle the top with the 4 tbsp. (60 mL) each bread crumbs and Parmesan. Bake 35-50 minutes (the time will vary depending on the water content of the potatoes and onions) until it is bubbly, the cream is absorbed, and the top is a lovely golden brown.

Remove the dish from the oven and let stand 20 minutes before serving, to thicken the sauce.

GARDENER'S CHICKEN

This casserole, combining tender, versatile chicken with the earthy flavours of mushrooms and rutabagas, will have them asking for more. Let it take centre stage with a simple side dish like parsley boiled potatoes or fluffy steamed rice. Leftovers—if you have them!—are delicious reheated in the microwave. Serves 3-4.

3-3 1/2 lbs.	chicken pieces	1.5-1.75 kg
4	slices bacon, chopped	4
2	large onions, sliced	2
2	stalks celery, sliced	2
1/2 cup	chopped rutabaga	125 mL
1/2 cup	sliced mushrooms	125 mL
2 tbsp.	butter or oil	30 mL
2 tbsp.	chopped fresh parsley	30 mL
1 tsp.	*each* dried tarragon and basil	5 mL
1	14 oz. (398 mL) can tomatoes	398 mL
	salt and pepper to taste	
	chopped fresh parsley for garnish	

Place the chicken pieces in a microproof casserole, arranging the thicker parts towards the outside edge of the dish.

Place the bacon, onions, celery, rutabaga, mushrooms, and butter in a microproof dish. Cover and microwave on HIGH 100% power 5-8 minutes until the vegetables are soft, stirring once during the cooking time. Blend in the herbs and tomatoes. Season with salt and black pepper and pour the mixture over the chicken pieces.

Cover and microwave on MEDIUM HIGH 70% power, allowing 6-8 minutes per pound (500 g) of chicken. Rearrange the chicken pieces halfway through the cooking time and baste well with sauce. Let the casserole stand, covered, for about 10 minutes after baking.

Top each chicken portion with sauce, sprinkle on a little chopped parsley, and serve.

C HICKEN-MUSHROOM LINGUINI

Buttered noodles give a truly authentic Italian touch to this creamy, quickly prepared chicken casserole. While it bakes, mix up a green or tomato salad, heat a few whole-grain dinner rolls, and your Italian evening meal is complete. Serves 4.

2	whole boneless chicken breasts	2
	(about 1 lb. (500 g))	
2 tbsp.	all-purpose flour	30 mL
1/2 tsp.	salt	2 mL
1/4 tsp.	pepper	1 mL
1 tbsp.	vegetable oil	15 mL
5 tbsp.	butter	75 mL
1	medium onion, finely chopped	1
2	cloves garlic, crushed	2
1 cup	chicken stock	250 mL
2 cups	small whole mushrooms, halved	500 mL
	(about 5 oz. (150 g))	
1 1/2 tbsp.	tomato paste	20 mL
1/2 tsp.	dried mixed herbs	2 mL
3 oz.	Black Forest ham, cut in thin strips	100 g
1	12 oz. (350 g) pkg. fresh linguini	1
1/2 cup	grated Parmesan cheese	125 mL
	chopped fresh parsley for garnish	

Heat the oven to 350°F (180°C).

Cut each chicken breast in half. Place the flour on a large plate and mix in the salt and pepper. Coat the chicken pieces in the seasoned flour.

In a large skillet, heat the oil and 1 tbsp. (15 mL) of the butter. Add the chicken and sauté over medium heat for about 10 minutes, turning until brown on both sides. Place in an 8 cup (2 L) casserole dish.

Add the onion and garlic to the skillet and sauté 2 minutes, until soft but not brown. Stir in any remaining seasoned flour. Blend in the stock, and bring it to a boil, stirring. Reduce the heat and stir in the mushrooms, tomato paste, and herbs. Pour the sauce over the chicken, cover and bake 30-35 minutes, until the chicken is cooked.

Remove from the oven and sprinkle the ham over the chicken. Return to the oven and bake, uncovered, 5 minutes longer.

During the last few minutes of cooking time, prepare the linguini according to the package directions. Drain well and toss with the Parmesan and the remaining 4 tbsp. (60 mL) butter.

Sprinkle the finished casserole with parsley and serve with the hot linguini.

CRANBERRY-PECAN CHICKEN DINNER

Everything cooks together in this family dinner recipe—plump chicken stuffed with a nutty cranberry stuffing, on a bed of colourful vegetables. Cooking it casserole-style makes the meat wonderfully moist, and you can substitute any of your favourite root vegetables, such as turnip, potato, or rutabaga. Serves 4.

1/2 lb.	sausage meat	250 g
1	large shallot, peeled and finely chopped	1
1/3 cup	chopped pecans	75 mL
1 tbsp.	chopped fresh parsley	15 mL
1/3 cup + 4 tbsp.	cranberry sauce	135 mL
1	3 lb. (1.5 kg) roasting or frying chicken	1
1	1 lb. (500 g) sweet potato, peeled and cut into 8 chunks	1
2	carrots, peeled and cut into 1 inch (2.5 cm) thick slices	2
2	parsnips, peeled and cut into 1 inch (2.5 cm) thick slices	2
1 1/2 cups	chicken stock	375 mL
	salt and pepper to taste	
1 1/2 tbsp.	margarine or butter	20 mL
2 tbsp.	all-purpose flour	30 mL

Heat the oven to 350°F (180°C).

In a skillet, sauté the sausage meat about 4 minutes over medium heat, stirring to break it up. Drain off most of the fat, then add the shallot and pecans and sauté for 2 minutes. Remove from the heat and stir in the parsley and 1/3 cup (75 mL) of the cranberry sauce. Allow to cool slightly.

Stuff the chicken with the sausage meat stuffing. Place the sweet potato, carrots, and parsnips in a 3 quart (3 L) casserole dish, then place the chicken on top. Pour over the stock and sprinkle the chicken with salt and pepper to taste. Cover and bake for 1 1/2 hours, then remove the cover and bake 30 minutes longer, uncovered, to brown the chicken. When cooked, the chicken should appear to pull away from the bones. Place the chicken and vegetables in a serving dish, cover, and keep warm. Strain off the stock into a measuring jug. Skim off any surface fat with a spoon. Add water if necessary until you have 1 1/2 cups (375 mL) stock. Set aside.

In a small saucepan, melt the margarine. Add the flour and cook 1 minute until pale golden brown. Remove from the heat and gradually stir in the stock. Return to the heat and bring to a boil, stirring, until thickened and smooth. Stir in the remaining 4 tbsp. (60 mL) cranberry sauce and heat through, stirring. Season to taste with salt and pepper. Serve the sauce with the chicken and vegetables.

The Easy Gourmet features a photograph of this recipe on page 71.

TURKEY RATATOUILLE

Ratatouille, the classic French mixed vegetable dish, turns up here as a wonderful partner to garlic-sautéed turkey breasts. Try this one at your next dinner party—easy to say, easy to cook, very easy to eat! Serve it hot and bubbly from the oven with steamed rice or fresh buttered noodles. Serves 6.

7-9 tbsp.	olive oil	105-135 mL
1	medium onion, sliced	1
2	large cloves garlic, crushed	2
1	1 lb. (500 g) eggplant, sliced	1
1	green bell pepper, sliced	1
1	red bell pepper, sliced	1
2	small zucchini, sliced	2
4	large tomatoes, peeled and sliced	4
1/3 cup	red wine or chicken stock	75 mL
1	bay leaf	1
	salt and pepper to taste	
3	boneless turkey breasts	3
	(about 1 1/2 lbs. (750 g))	
2 tbsp.	all-purpose flour	30 mL
1	clove garlic, crushed	1
2 cups	grated mozzarella cheese	500 mL

Heat 4 tbsp. (60 mL) of the oil in a large saucepan. Add the onion and garlic and sauté over medium heat about 3 minutes until soft but not brown. Add the eggplant and 3-4 more tablespoons of oil. Sauté about 5 minutes, until soft. Add the peppers and zucchini to the pan, with more oil if necessary. Sauté, stirring, for 2 minutes. Stir in the tomatoes, wine, and bay leaf. Cover and simmer for 30 minutes, until the mixture reaches a good thick consistency. Remove and discard the bay leaf. Season to taste with salt and pepper.

Heat the oven to 350°F (180°C). Cut each turkey breast into 4 pieces. Place the turkey between 2 sheets of waxed paper and beat with a meat mallet or rolling pin to half the original thickness. Place the flour on a plate and sprinkle with salt and pepper. Coat the turkey pieces in the seasoned flour. Heat 2 tbsp. (30 mL) of the oil in a large skillet. Add the garlic and sauté 30 seconds, stirring. Add the turkey and sauté about 5 minutes, or until cooked and golden brown on both sides.

Place the ratatouille mixture in a 9 x 13 inch (23 x 32 cm) ovenproof baking dish. Arrange the turkey in overlapping slices on top. Sprinkle on cheese to cover. Cover the dish and bake 25-35 minutes, or until heated through. Remove the cover and bake 10 minutes longer to brown.

RED SNAPPER MEXICANA

Preparing fresh fish for a crowd can be a challenge. But this oven-baked Mexican-inspired way with fresh red snapper fillets is perfect for a large group. Baked in a handsome oven-to-table baking dish and loaded with fresh leeks, diced chiles, olives, and lots of spicy seasonings, the dish needs only some rice, warm corn tortillas and butter, and a fresh avocado salad to complete your fiesta-style supper. Serves 8.

8	fresh red snapper fillets, 6-8 oz. (175-250 g) each	8
6 cups	sliced leeks	1.5 L
1/2 cup	olive oil	125 mL
1	onion, halved and thinly sliced	1
4	cloves garlic, slivered	4
1	1.25 oz. (35 g) pkg. taco seasoning mix	1
1	14 oz. (398 mL) can stewed tomatoes	1
2 tsp.	sugar	10 mL
1 tbsp.	sherry wine or red wine vinegar	15 mL
2	4 oz. (125 mL) cans diced roasted chiles	2
3 tbsp.	capers	45 mL
3/4 cup	sliced green pimiento-stuffed olives	175 mL
1 tsp.	dried oregano	5 mL
	salt and freshly ground black pepper to taste	

Rinse the fish under cold running water, drain, and pat completely dry. Slice the leeks into 1 1/2 x 1/2 inch (3.5 x 1 cm) julienne, using only the white and lighter green part of the leek.

In a very large skillet, saucepan, or wok, heat the olive oil over medium-high heat. Add the leeks and quickly sauté, stirring, until slightly tender and pale golden on the edges. Add the onion and garlic, increase the heat to high, and sauté until translucent, about 5 minutes.

Add the taco seasoning mix, stewed tomatoes with their juice, sugar, and vinegar. Cook the mixture quickly over the highest heat to evaporate most of the juices, so that the sauce is thick. Stir in the chiles, capers, olives, and oregano, and heat 2-3 minutes until bubbly.

Heat the oven to 375°F (190°C).

Line a 10 x 14 inch (25 x 35 cm) heavy baking dish with a sheet of baking parchment. Spoon a very thin, spare layer of the vegetables and sauce on the bottom of the lined dish. Roll each fillet in thirds, tucking the ends under, and place them over the vegetables. Season the fillets with salt and pepper. Divide remaining vegetable mixture and mound on top of each fillet to cover.

Bake the assembled dish, uncovered, in the centre of the oven 30 minutes, no more. Remove from the oven and allow to rest 20-30 minutes before serving for the juices to thicken and the flavours to blend. Serve warm, one portion per serving, lifting up each portion with a flat metal spatula. Serve a spoonful of the pan juices alongside each serving.

SHRIMP-CRAB-MUSHROOM QUICHE

Even real men will eat this quiche! Spinach salad or a ready-made green salad from the deli rounds out the meal. Serves 6.

1	9 inch (23 cm) deep-dish frozen pastry pie shell	1
1 1/2 tbsp.	margarine or butter	20 mL
1 1/2 cups	thinly sliced mushrooms	375 mL
4	large green onions, thinly sliced	4
1	2 oz. (60 g) can crab meat, drained	1
4 oz.	fresh cooked shrimp	125 g
3/4 cup	grated Swiss cheese	175 mL
2	large eggs	2
3/4 cup	half-and-half cream	175 mL
pinch	ground nutmeg	pinch
1/4 tsp.	*each* salt and pepper	1 mL

Heat the oven to 425°F (220°C). With a fork, lightly prick the bottom of the pastry in several places. Line with foil and bake on a cookie sheet for 10 minutes. Remove the foil and bake 3 minutes longer. Remove the shell from the oven and cool. Reduce the oven temperature to 350°F (180°C).

In a small skillet, melt the margarine. Add the mushrooms and green onions and sauté 1 minute over medium heat. Lift out of the pan with a slotted spoon and scatter over the bottom of the pastry shell. Sprinkle on the crab and shrimp and then the cheese.

In a medium bowl, beat the eggs. Stir in the cream, nutmeg, salt, and pepper. Pour the cream mixture into the pastry shell. Bake 35-40 minutes or until the filling is golden and firm.

The Easy Gourmet features a photograph of this recipe on page 53.

CREOLE JAMBALAYA

Jambalaya is one of the best rice dishes in the world. This is a quick, everyday version, loaded with chicken, sausage and shellfish, flavoured with traditional Louisiana ingredients. Serve with a hot loaf of French bread, and don't forget to put a bottle of hot pepper sauce on the table for an authentic finishing touch. Serves 4-6.

6 tbsp.	olive oil	90 mL
2 1/2 lbs.	chicken drumsticks and thighs	1.25 Kg
	salt, pepper, paprika, and dried thyme to taste	
1	large onion, chopped	1
1	*each* green and red bell pepper, diced	1
4	stalks celery, diced	4
1	bunch green onions, sliced	1
2	cloves garlic, crushed	2
2	bay leaves	2
1 1/2 tsp.	*each* dried thyme and salt	7 mL
1/2 tsp.	*each* ground allspice and cayenne pepper	2 mL
2 tsp.	paprika	10 mL
2 cups	long-grain white rice	500 mL
1	28 oz. (796 mL) can stewed tomatoes, including liquid	1
2 1/2 cups	chicken stock	625 mL
1 lb.	smoked sausage (garlic coil, Mennonite, Ukrainian)	500 g
	sliced 3/4 inch (2 cm) thick	
12	fresh clams, in the shell	12
12	fresh mussels, in the shell	12
12	large Tiger prawns, in the shell, legs removed, tails intact	12
	bottled hot pepper sauce	
	lemon wedges and minced parsley for garnish (optional)	

Heat 2 tbsp. (30 mL) of the olive oil in a large, deep, heavy skillet over medium-high heat. Brown the chicken pieces and cook 10 minutes on each side, seasoning liberally with salt, pepper, paprika, and thyme as they cook. Transfer the chicken to a platter, discard drippings, and wipe the skillet clean.

Heat the remaining 4 tbsp. (60 mL) oil in the same skillet. Add the onion, pepper, celery, and green onions. Sauté, stirring, over medium-high heat until the vegetables are softened and pale golden, about 15 minutes. Add the garlic, bay leaves, thyme, salt, allspice, cayenne, and paprika and sauté 4-5 minutes. Stir in the rice and sauté 3-4 minutes until the rice glistens and is translucent and coated with oil.

Add the tomatoes, their liquid, and the chicken broth. Bring to a boil. Reduce the heat so that the liquid simmers. Tuck in the browned chicken pieces so they are half covered with rice. Cover and cook 20 minutes, until almost all the liquid is absorbed.

Uncover and add the sausage, clams, mussels, and prawns, tucking them in so they are halfway covered with rice. Cover and cook about 10 minutes until the shellfish open, the shrimp is opaque and just firm, and the rice is cooked. Uncover and allow the dish to rest 10 minutes before serving.

Fluff the rice with a fork. Serve the Jambalaya at once with a shaker of hot pepper sauce, fresh lemon wedges, and a scattering of minced parsley if desired.

The Easy Gourmet features a photograph of this recipe on the front cover.

SALMON TERIYAKI CASSEROLE

Here is a dish for salmon lovers—delicately seasoned, with a tangy touch of the Orient. The bonus is there is no pre-cooking. Just arrange everything in a casserole dish and bake. The dish is ideal for quick, elegant entertaining, served with hot fluffy rice and fresh steamed snow peas. Serves 4.

3/4 cup	soy sauce	175 mL
1/2 cup	honey	125 mL
3 tbsp.	vegetable oil	45 mL
3 tbsp.	fresh lemon juice	45 mL
3	cloves garlic, crushed	3
3/4 tsp.	ground ginger	4 mL
4	salmon fillets, skinned and halved lengthwise (about 1 lb. (500 g))	4
1	medium red bell pepper, thinly sliced	1
6 oz.	mushrooms, sliced (about 2 cups (500 mL))	150 g
6	green onions, diagonally sliced	6
1 1/2 tbsp.	cornstarch	20 mL
1 1/2 tbsp.	water	20 mL

In a shallow casserole dish large enough to hold the salmon fillets in a single layer, combine the soy sauce, honey, vegetable oil, lemon juice, garlic, and ginger, mixing well. Place the salmon in the marinade, turning to coat. Cover and marinate in the refrigerator 30 minutes.

Heat the oven to 400°F (200°C). Sprinkle the red pepper, mushrooms, and green onions over the salmon. Baste with the marinade. Bake, uncovered, 20 minutes, basting occasionally, or until the fish is tender when flaked with a fork. Remove from the oven and lift out the salmon with a slotted spoon into a warm serving dish. Keep warm.

Pour the sauce into a saucepan. Blend the cornstarch with the water, stir into the sauce and bring it to a boil, stirring, until the mixture thickens. Pour the sauce over the salmon and serve at once.

Opposite: Cranberry-Pecan Chicken Dinner (p. 62).

REAMY PAPRIKA HALIBUT

Wrapped in cream and spiked delicately with paprika, this easy casserole makes a terrific main course. Serve it with lemon-flavoured rice and a mound of steaming fresh microwaved green beans, or on its own, in smaller portions, as a seafood lovers' appetizer. Serves 4-6.

2 tbsp.	butter	30 mL
2 tbsp.	finely chopped onion	30 mL
1/2 cup	sliced fresh mushrooms	125 mL
2 lbs.	halibut, skin and bones removed	1 kg
2 tbsp.	lemon juice	30 mL
1 cup	whipping cream	250 mL
1 tbsp.	paprika	15 mL
4 oz.	cooked shrimp	125 g
	lemon wedges and parsley for garnish	

Place the butter, onion, and mushrooms in a microproof casserole dish. Cover and microwave on HIGH 100% power 2-4 minutes until the vegetables are soft.

Cut the halibut into serving-size pieces and add to the onion mixture in the casserole dish. Add the lemon juice.

Cover and microwave on HIGH 100% power 4-8 minutes until the halibut is cooked, spooning the vegetables over the fish halfway through the cooking time.

Add the cream and dust with paprika. Cover and microwave on MEDIUM 50% power 2-4 minutes until the cream is heated through. Add the shrimp, cover, and microwave on MEDIUM 50% power 1 minute longer to heat the shrimp through.

Serve garnished with lemon and parsley.

ROVENÇAL FISH FILLETS

This savoury, succulent recipe for oven-baked fresh fish fillets is a snap to assemble, fun to prepare, dazzling in colour, and low in fat and calories to boot! Try it with fresh red snapper, sole, or cod. Serve with linguini or spaghettini dusted with Parmesan cheese and a hot loaf of sourdough bread. Serves 6.

6	fresh fillets of red snapper, sole or thick-cut pieces of fresh cod (about 2 lbs. (1 kg))	6
4	large leeks	4
2	orange or yellow bell peppers	2
4	stalks celery, including leaves	4
6 tbsp.	olive oil	90 mL
1	14 oz. (398 mL) can stewed tomatoes, including juice	1
1 tsp.	*each* dried thyme and sugar	5 mL
1 tbsp.	*each* capers and green peppercorns	15 mL
2 tbsp.	fresh lemon juice	30 mL
1	lemon, cut into paper-thin slices, including rind	1
	garlic seasoning salt to taste	
	freshly ground black pepper to taste	

Rinse the fish fillets under cold water briefly, drain, and gently pat dry. Discard the tough darker green ends of the leeks, rinse well, and slice lengthwise into julienne strips 1/2 inch (1 cm) wide x 2 inches (5 cm) long. Stem and seed the peppers and slice into thin julienne strips. Slice the celery crosswise into 1/4 inch (6 mm) pieces.

In a large wok or skillet, heat the olive oil over high heat until sizzling. Add the leeks, celery, and peppers and quickly stir-fry to coat the vegetables and soften slightly, 6-7 minutes. Add the stewed tomatoes and their liquid, increase the heat to high, and quickly cook, stirring, to reduce the juices to several tablespoons. Season the mixture with thyme, sugar, capers, green peppercorns, and lemon juice. Sauté 1-2 minutes longer to evaporate most of the juices. Do not overcook the vegetables, as they should remain tender-crisp and bright in colour. Set aside several minutes. Heat the oven to 375°F (190°C).

Line a heavy rectangular 10 x 14 inch (25 x 35 cm) baking dish with a sheet of baking parchment. Lay the sliced lemons on the paper. Spoon a small amount of the vegetable mixture over the lemons as a bed for the fish.

Gently roll each fish fillet into thirds, tucking both ends under, and place the fillets over the vegetables, seam side down, smooth side up. Season the fillets with garlic salt and pepper. Divide the remaining vegetable mixture and mound it on each fillet to cover. Place the dish in the centre of the oven and bake exactly 30 minutes (no more!). Remove the dish from the oven, and allow to rest 20 minutes before serving for the juices to thicken slightly. Serve warm, room temperature, or even chilled the next day. Lift each portion from the dish with a flat metal spatula and serve a spoonful of the pan juices alongside each serving.

The Easy Gourmet features a photograph of this recipe on page 107.

TUNA CASSEROLE WITH A TWIST

Here is a light supper dish, easy to prepare, attractive on the table, and a nutritious variation on a family favourite. Serve with hot buttered chunks of Batter Corn Bread (p. 150) and your favourite green salad. Serves 2-3.

1 cup	long-grain rice, cooked	250 mL
1	10 oz. (284 mL) can golden mushroom soup	1
1/2 cup	milk	125 mL
1	7 oz. (198 g) can solid white tuna, drained	1
1/2	small red bell pepper, diced	1/2
15	snow peas, cut diagonally into thirds	15
1 tbsp.	crushed dried chile pepper	15 mL
	freshly ground black pepper to taste	
	juice of 1 lemon	
	chow mein noodles and lemon twists for garnish	

Mix together the cooked rice, soup, milk, tuna, red pepper, and snow peas. Season to taste with the crushed chiles, black pepper, and lemon juice.

Spoon the mixture into a greased ovenproof casserole. Bake, covered, at 375°F (190°C) until bubbling and heated through, about 35 minutes.

Top with chow mein noodles and a twist of lemon, and serve.

VEGETABLE LASAGNE

Lasagne was never was so easy! "Oven-ready" lasagne noodles, found near the packaged dry pasta, mean no muss and no fuss—just lay the dry noodles in the casserole dish and they cook as they bake. And there are so many flavourful vegetables and cheeses packed into this dish, you'll never miss the meat. Serves 8.

2 tbsp.	vegetable oil	30 mL
1	large onion, chopped	1
1	red bell pepper, thinly sliced	1
2	cloves garlic, crushed	2
1	28 oz. (796 mL) can tomatoes	1
3	large carrots, peeled and sliced	3
2	large leeks, sliced	2
2 cups	sliced mushrooms	500 mL
2	medium zucchini, sliced	2
1/3 cup	tomato paste	75 mL
1/2 tsp.	*each* dried mixed herbs and salt	2 mL
1/4 tsp.	pepper	1 mL
12	pieces "oven-ready" lasagne	12
1	8 oz. (250 g) carton ricotta cheese	1
3/4 cup	grated Parmesan cheese	175 mL
1	7 oz. (227 g) package mozzarella cheese, grated	1

In a large saucepan, heat the vegetable oil. Add the onion, pepper, and garlic and sauté about 4 minutes, until soft but not brown. Add the tomatoes, carrots, leeks, mushrooms, zucchini, tomato paste, and mixed herbs. Bring to a boil, then cover and simmer 1 hour. Remove the lid and cook over medium heat 15 minutes, to thicken the sauce. Stir in the salt and pepper.

Heat the oven to 350°F (180°C). In a lightly buttered casserole dish, wide and long enough to take 4 of the lasagne noodles in a single layer, spread a thin layer of the vegetables. Lay 4 noodles on top in a single layer. Layer on a third of the vegetables, a third of the ricotta, a third of the Parmesan, and a third of the mozzarella. Add two more layers, finishing with mozzarella.

Cover and bake for 40 minutes, until the lasagne is tender. Uncover for the last 5 minutes of cooking time to brown the top slightly.

MUSTARD SCALLOPED POTATOES

This special potato casserole deserves a special occasion. So offer it with the Thanksgiving turkey instead of the more conventional roast potatoes, or substitute milk for the cream and omit the garlic for a lighter side dish. Any way you fix it, this one is a winner as part of a dinner of meat, fish, or poultry and seasonal green vegetables. Serves 6.

1 cup	half-and-half cream	250 mL
1 tbsp.	Dijon mustard	15 mL
2 tbsp.	chopped fresh parsley or chives	30 mL
1/4 tsp.	*each* salt and pepper	1 mL
3 tbsp.	softened butter	45 mL
1	large clove garlic, crushed	1
4	large potatoes, peeled and thinly sliced	4
1	large onion, thinly sliced	1
1 cup	grated Swiss cheese	250 mL

Heat the oven to 350°F (180°C).

In a small bowl, blend together the cream and mustard. Stir in the parsley, salt, and pepper. In another small bowl, beat together the butter and garlic.

Arrange a quarter of the potato slices in overlapping layers in an 8 cup (2 L) lightly buttered casserole dish. Dot with a quarter of the garlic butter. Layer on a third of the onion slices and sprinkle with a third of the cheese. Repeat, layering twice more and finishing with an overlapping layer of the potatoes. Dot with the remaining garlic butter and pour the cream mixture over the top.

Bake, covered, for 1 hour. Remove the cover and bake 30-45 minutes longer, until the potatoes are cooked and the top is golden brown.

Note: Do not prepare this casserole too far in advance of cooking, as the potatoes may discolour.

MUSHROOM SPOONBREAD PUDDING

This lovely mushroom-studded cheese bread pudding makes a homey, comforting Sunday night supper. Serve it with a crisp green salad with slivers of avocado and red onion, and big goblets of cold sparkling cider. Serves 6.

1 lb.	fresh mushrooms, caps tightly closed, wiped clean (not washed) and sliced	500 g
6 tbsp.	butter	90 mL
6	extra-large eggs	6
1/2 cup	*each* milk and whipping cream	125 mL
1/4 tsp.	ground nutmeg	1 mL
2 tbsp.	minced fresh parsley	30 mL
	salt and freshly ground black pepper to taste	
8	3/4 inch (2 cm) thick slices firm white bread, crusts removed, cubed	8
8 oz.	*each* sharp Canadian cheddar cheese and imported Swiss cheese, cubed	250 g
8 oz.	Black Forest or banquet ham, cubed	250 g

In a large skillet over medium-high heat, sauté the sliced mushrooms in the butter until tender-crisp and golden brown. Sauté them very quickly so that the juices are not released. The mushrooms must be very dry. Set the skillet aside to cool the mushrooms completely.

Heat the oven to 350°F (180°C) (if baking in glass, heat the oven to 325°F [160°C]). Generously butter the bottom and sides of an 8 x 10 inch (20 x 25 cm) baking dish.

Whip the eggs with the milk and cream until frothy. Season the egg mixture with the nutmeg, parsley, salt, and liberal grindings of pepper. Fold in the bread, cheeses, and ham. Fold in the cooled mushrooms. Immediately pour the mixture into the baking dish. If any egg mixture is left in the bowl, drizzle it over the top evenly.

Bake the pudding about 45 minutes, or until the cheese bubbles, the pudding has puffed, and the top is golden brown all over. Remove the pudding from the oven and let it rest 5 minutes. Serve each portion with a large serving spoon onto warmed plates.

GARDEN PIE

A cornucopia of fresh late summer vegetables and two creamy cheeses, all spiked with mint and wrapped in flaky golden pastry—what could be more satisfying on a cool autumn evening? Served with your favourite Hollandaise sauce, this dish is nutritious, tasty, and just plain good eating. Serves 6.

4 tbsp.	oil	60 mL
2	medium Japanese eggplant, sliced 1/4 inch (6 mm) thick	2
1	medium onion, chopped	1
5	green onions, chopped	5
3	stalks celery, chopped	3
1	small red bell pepper, chopped	1
5	medium mushrooms, sliced	5
2	cloves garlic, minced	2
4 cups	fresh spinach leaves, about 1 bunch	1 L
1/2 cup	grated cheddar cheese	125 mL
1/2 cup	grated mozzarella cheese	125 mL
1 tbsp.	chopped fresh mint	15 mL
	salt and pepper to taste	
3	eggs, well beaten	3
1	7 1/2 oz. (215 g) pkg. regular or puff pastry	1

Heat 2 tbsp. (30 mL) of the oil in a large skillet and quickly cook the sliced eggplant. Remove it from the pan and layer it in the bottom of a 9 inch (23 cm) oiled ovenproof quiche dish or pie plate.

Add the remaining 2 tbsp. (30 mL) of oil to the skillet and sauté the two kinds of onion, celery, and red pepper for 2 minutes longer. Add the mushrooms and garlic and cook 2 minutes. Add the spinach leaves. Cover the skillet and steam 2-3 minutes. Spoon the mixture into the prepared pan. Scatter on the cheeses, mint, and seasonings. Reserving 1 tbsp. (15 mL) of the beaten egg, pour the remainder over the vegetable cheese mixture, spreading evenly. Let cool.

Heat the oven to 400°F (200°C). Roll out the pastry into a 10 inch (25 cm) circle and lightly score a pattern on top with the tines of a fork. Lay it over the cooled vegetable mixture. Brush with the reserved egg. Bake the pie until puffed and very golden brown, about 35-40 minutes. Serve hot.

STEWS

What could be more welcoming than the aroma of homemade stew on a cool autumn evening? Serve up steaming bowls of Chunky Prairie Stew or Spiced Chicken Stew with Apricots and watch them come back for more! Having a party? Try Seafood Stew with Saffron or Party Time Chorizo Chili. Warm, filling, and loaded with the hearty flavours of autumn, stew is the perfect dish for fall weather.

ED BEAN COWBOY CHILI

This hearty one-dish wonder serves a big group of hungry chili-lovers. It's great off the stove, but even better made the day before and reheated. Either way, round out the dinner with a cast-iron pan of hot corn bread and a big wooden bowl of green salad. Serves 6-8.

4 tbsp.	olive oil	60 mL
3 lbs.	ground beef	1.5 kg
4 tbsp.	bacon drippings	60 mL
3 cups	diced onion	750 mL
4	cloves garlic, crushed	4
3 tbsp.	chili powder	45 mL
2-3 tsp.	salt	10-15 mL
3 tbsp.	*each* brown sugar and red wine vinegar	45 mL
1 tbsp.	*each* ground cumin, cinnamon, and cloves	15 mL
1 tbsp.	dried oregano	15 mL
1 tbsp.	paprika	15 mL
1	6 oz. (100 mL) can tomato paste	100 mL
12 oz.	dark beer or ale	180 mL
1	28 oz. (796 mL) can crushed tomatoes	1
3	14-oz. (398 mL) cans red kidney beans, drained	3
	freshly ground black pepper to taste	
	grated cheddar cheese and minced red or green onions for garnish (optional)	

Heat the olive oil in a very heavy, large Dutch oven or cast-iron pot. Add the ground beef, and sauté over high heat, stirring to break up the meat, until lightly browned. Drain off the excess fat. In a skillet, heat the bacon drippings over medium-high heat, and add the onions. Sauté, stirring, until golden. Add the garlic and sauté 2 minutes. Scrape the onions and drippings into the browned meat.

Bring the mixture to a bubbly simmer over medium-high heat. Stir in the chili powder, salt, brown sugar, vinegar, cumin, cinnamon, cloves, oregano, and paprika. Heat until bubbly, thickened, and very glossy, about 6 minutes, stirring. Combine the tomato paste and beer and add it to the simmering meat mixture with the crushed tomatoes.

Partially cover the pot and simmer the chili 2-3 hours, stirring every half hour. Add the drained kidney beans and pepper, and cook 45 minutes longer, uncovered, until thick and glossy. Taste and correct for seasonings. Serve piping hot in deep crockery bowls, topped with grated cheddar and minced red or green onions if desired.

Note: If you prepare the chili the day before, add the beans just before re-heating for 45 minutes. The beans will retain their texture and shape better if they are added at this point.

The Easy Gourmet features a photograph of this recipe on page 89.

MEATBALL AND CHICKPEA CHILI STEW

The cooking of Africa inspired this dish, a blend of intriguing spices and meat with a medley of vegetables. The stew is full of flavour and fibre, and needs only fluffy rice to complete the meal. Serves 4.

CHICKPEA CHILI STEW

3 tbsp.	vegetable oil	45 mL
1	large onion, chopped	1
1	large clove garlic, crushed	1
1	*each* large leek and carrot, sliced	1
1	*each* parsnip and potato, peeled and diced	1
2	large tomatoes, cored and chopped	2
2 cups	chicken stock	500 mL
3 tbsp.	tomato paste	45 mL
1 tbsp.	chili powder	15 mL
1 tsp.	cumin powder	5 mL
1/2 tsp.	*each* turmeric and dried thyme	2 mL
1	19 oz. (540 mL) can chickpeas, drained	1
	salt and pepper to taste	

MEATBALLS

3/4 lb.	ground beef	375 g
1/2 cup	finely chopped onion	125 mL
1	large clove garlic, crushed	1
1/4 tsp.	*each* salt and pepper	1 mL
1 tbsp.	all-purpose flour	15 mL
1 1/2 tbsp.	vegetable oil	20 mL

To make the stew, heat the oil in a large saucepan. Add the onion and garlic and sauté over medium heat 3 minutes until soft but not brown. Add the leek, carrot, parsnip, and potato. Sauté 2 minutes, stirring. Add the tomatoes, stock, tomato paste, chili, cumin, turmeric, and thyme. Cover and simmer 20-25 minutes, until the vegetables are cooked. Stir in the chickpeas and cook 5 minutes. Season with salt and pepper.

Meanwhile, make the meatballs. In a medium bowl, combine the ground beef, onion, garlic, salt, and pepper. Form into 16 small balls. Roll each ball in the flour. Heat the oil in a large skillet and fry the meatballs for about 10 minutes or until cooked, turning often. Serve the stew in a shallow serving dish and mound the meatballs on top.

 # HUNKY PRAIRIE STEW

This traditional hearty beef stew gets its comforting taste from a simple blend of fresh vegetables and rich, tender chunks of beef. Just add a big, steaming bowl of creamy mashed potatoes. Serves 6.

1 1/2 lbs.	stew beef, trimmed, cut into 1 inch (2.5 cm) cubes	750 g
3 tbsp.	all-purpose flour	45 mL
1/2 tsp.	salt	2 mL
1/4 tsp.	pepper	1 mL
2 tbsp.	margarine	30 mL
1	large onion, thinly sliced	1
1	10 oz. (284 mL) can beef broth	1
3/4 cup	water	175 mL
2	medium potatoes, peeled and cut into 1 inch (2.5 cm) chunks	2
2	large carrots, peeled and sliced 1/2 inch (1 cm) thick	2
1	large parsnip, peeled and cut into 1 inch (2.5 cm) chunks	1
3 cups	rutabaga in 1 inch (2.5 cm) chunks	750 mL
1	bay leaf	1
1/2 tsp.	dried mixed herbs	2 mL

Toss the beef with the flour, salt, and pepper until coated. Melt the margarine in a large saucepan. Add the beef and onion and sauté over medium heat about 4 minutes, or until the meat loses its pink colour, scraping the bottom of the pan occasionally. Pour in the broth and water and bring to a boil, stirring. Reduce the heat to low. Add the potatoes, carrots, parsnip, rutabaga, bay leaf, and mixed herbs. Cover and simmer 1 1/2-2 hours or until the meat is tender, stirring occasionally. Serve hot.

PARTY TIME CHORIZO CHILI

This chili deserves a party—it's that good! Chock full of savoury black beans, chunky beef, and spicy chorizo sausage, this one is meant to be ladled up into huge bowls, topped with chopped red onions and a squeeze of fresh lime, and enjoyed. Serves 8.

3 cups	dried black beans, rinsed	750 mL
1/3 cup	olive oil or vegetable oil	75 mL
2 cups	coarsely diced onion	500 mL
2	red bell peppers, diced	2
2	cloves garlic, minced	2
2 lbs.	ground beef	1 kg
2 tbsp.	chili power	30 mL
2 tbsp.	paprika	30 mL
1/2 tsp.	cayenne pepper	2 mL
2 tsp.	salt	10 mL
2 tsp.	cracked black pepper	10 mL
1 tbsp.	ground cumin	15 mL
2 tbsp.	dried oregano	30 mL
2 tsp.	liquid smoke	10 mL
2	bay leaves	2
1	12 oz. (375 mL) bottle prepared chili sauce	1
1	14 oz. (398 mL) can crushed tomatoes	1
1 cup	rich beef stock or beer	250 mL
1 1/2 lbs.	chorizo sausage (or substitute any other smoked, cooked firm sausage), sliced into 1/2 inch (1 cm) rounds	750 g
1/2 cup	dried currants, rinsed in warm water and drained	125 mL
	bottled hot pepper sauce to taste	
	fresh lime wedges and finely diced red onion for garnish	

Cook the beans in cold water, according to package directions, for 2 1/2-3 hours or just until tender (do not overcook, or beans will lose their shape). Set aside.

Heat the oil over medium-high heat in a very large Dutch oven. Add the onions and peppers and sauté until softened. Stir in the garlic and beef. Increase the heat to high and sauté, breaking the meat up with a spoon, until the beef is no longer pink. Season the meat mixture with the chili powder, paprika, cayenne, salt, pepper, cumin, oregano, liquid smoke, and bay leaves. Cook, stirring, 15 minutes to flavour the meat. Add the chili sauce, crushed tomatoes, and beef stock and bring the mixture to a bubbly simmer.

Reduce the heat to medium-low, partially cover, and cook 2-3 hours, stirring every half hour. Add the sausage, currants, and cooked black beans. Simmer the chili 35 minutes longer until thick and glossy. Taste and correct for seasonings, adding a healthy dash or two of hot pepper sauce.

Ladle the chili into deep bowls, each serving garnished with a wedge of fresh lime and a spoonful of chopped red onion.

DOUBLE-OLIVE MEDITERRANEAN BEEF STEW

Visitors to the French Riviera in southern France leave with delicious memories of the fragrant meat and fish stews so popular in that part of the world. This one, a provençal daube (meat stew) is spicy, heady with red wine, and packed with the flavour of two kinds of olives. Serve it with pasta or rice and lots of warm French baguette to dip into the savoury sauce. A cooling compote of fresh oranges sprinkled with cinnamon-sugar and burnt almonds makes a great finish to this lovely meal. Serves 8.

4 lbs.	stew beef, cut into 1 1/2 inch (3.5 cm) cubes	2 kg
4-6	cloves garlic, crushed	4-6
3 cups	dry red wine	750 mL
1/2 tsp.	*each* ground cinnamon and cloves	2 mL
4	bay leaves, crumbled	4
2 tsp.	dried thyme	10 mL
1 tbsp.	sugar	15 mL
1 tbsp.	red wine vinegar	15 mL
1	continuous 5 inch (13 cm) spiral *each* orange and lemon rind	1
2-3 tsp.	salt	10-15 mL
6 oz.	thick-sliced bacon, cut into 1/2 inch (1 cm) pieces	180 g
1 tbsp.	*each* butter and olive oil	15 mL
2	large onions, halved and sliced	2
4	large carrots, scraped and sliced into 1/4 inch (6 mm) thick rounds	4
1 lb.	Roma tomatoes, halved and cut into 1/2 inch (1 cm) thick slices	500 g
1 cup	black kalamata olives	250 mL
1 cup	green olives	250 mL
1/3 cup	minced fresh parsley	75 mL

Marinate the beef overnight, refrigerated, in the garlic, red wine, cinnamon, cloves, bay leaves, thyme, sugar, vinegar, citrus rinds, and salt.

Heat a large, heavy Dutch oven with a very tight-fitting lid and sauté the bacon with the butter and olive oil, stirring, until the bacon is translucent and pale golden. Add the onions and carrots and sauté until the vegetables are slightly tender and pale golden on the edges. Add the tomatoes and heat until bubbly. Stir in the olives.

Add the meat and all the marinade, stir to combine with the bacon and vegetables, and bring the stew to a simmer. Place a double sheet of foil under the pot lid to seal, cover tightly, and simmer the stew over the lowest heat so that it barely "shimmers." Cook the stew for 4-5 hours. Don't take the lid off.

Take the stew to the table, remove the lid and the foil, and let the entire family enjoy the wonderful aroma as it rises from the pot. Sprinkle with parsley and serve at once.

The Easy Gourmet features a photograph of this recipe on page 35.

OLISH BIGOS STEW

Bigos is a wonderful stew, needing only a warm, crusty loaf of hearty whole grain or rye bread and a crock of butter to complete the meal. Serves 8-10.

4 tbsp.	vegetable oil or bacon drippings	60 mL
1	very large onion, coarsely chopped	1
2	large cloves garlic, minced	2
2	large tart green apples, peeled and coarsely diced	2
1 tbsp.	brown sugar	15 mL
1 tbsp.	sweet Hungarian paprika	15 mL
2 tsp.	whole caraway seeds	10 mL
1 lb.	boneless pork, cut into 1 inch (2.5 cm) cubes	500 g
1 lb.	boneless veal, cut into 1 inch (2.5 cm) cubes	500 g
2 lbs.	smoked, cooked Polish or Ukrainian-type sausage, sliced into 3/4 inch (2 cm) rounds	1 kg
1 cup	*each* apple cider and beef stock	250 mL
1 quart	sauerkraut, rinsed and drained	1 L
1	28 oz. (796 mL) can plum tomatoes, broken up, with liquid	1
2	bay leaves	2
1 tsp.	*each* salt and cracked black pepper	5 mL
1 cup	beer or ale	250 mL
1 cup	dried prunes	250 mL
1/3 cup	minced fresh parsley	75 mL
	sour cream for garnish (optional)	

Heat the oil in a very large Dutch oven over medium-high heat. Add the onion, garlic, and apples and sauté, stirring, until golden brown. Sprinkle with sugar and sauté 1 minute longer until bubbly. Add the paprika and caraway seeds, and sauté 2 minutes. Add the pork, veal, sausage, cider, beef stock, sauerkraut, tomatoes, bay leaves, salt, pepper, beer, and prunes. Bring the mixture to a simmer, cover, reduce the heat to low, and cook 2 hours. Stir, partially cover, and simmer 1 hour. Let the stew stand 1 hour before serving. Serve warm in large bowls. Top each portion with parsley and a dollop of sour cream.

Opposite: Red Bean Cowboy Chili (p. 80), Batter Corn Bread (p. 150).

NEW ORLEANS RED BEANS AND RICE

Louis Armstrong used to sign his autograph with a tongue-in-cheek "red beans and ricely yours," with good reason! Lush, savoury red beans, studded with smoked sausage, ladled over big bowls of steamy white rice—the combination is unbeatable. Serves 8.

2 lbs.	red (kidney) beans, soaked in cold water overnight	1 kg
1	bunch green onions, sliced	1
1	small green pepper, diced	1
3	large cloves garlic, minced	3
1	medium onion, diced	1
2	ham hocks, cracked in several places	2
2 tsp.	salt	10 mL
2	bay leaves	2
3 tbsp.	molasses	45 mL
1 tsp.	*each* dried thyme, oregano, and black pepper	5 mL
1/4 tsp.	cayenne pepper	1 mL
2 quarts	cold water (as needed)	2 L
3 tbsp.	red wine vinegar	45 mL
1 lb.	smoked sausage	500 g
	(garlic coil, Mennonite, Ukrainian, or smoked deli-style knockwurst), sliced into 1/2 inch (1 cm) thick rounds	
8 cups	hot cooked long-grain rice	2 L
2 cups	thinly sliced green onions	500 mL
	bottled hot pepper sauce	

Drain the beans and place in a large, heavy stock pot. Add the green onions, green pepper, garlic, onion, ham hocks, salt, bay leaves, molasses, thyme, oregano, black pepper, and cayenne. Add enough of the cold water to just cover the mixture. Bring to a boil, then lower the heat and simmer the beans, partially covered, for 3 hours. Add the vinegar and sliced sausage during the final hour of cooking and, if the beans are dry, some additional water. Cook until the beans are tender and the sauce is thickened. Ladle the beans over mounds of rice in deep crockery bowls. Sprinkle with green onion and pass the hot pepper sauce!

HEARTY BEEF AND BACON BOURGUIGNON

This famous French-inspired beef stew deserves its reputation. Rich gravy, tiny carmelized onions, mushrooms, and bacon make this hearty stew delicious on the first day and every bit as good reheated the next day. Serve with a leafy green salad with toasted walnuts and a mustardy vinaigrette. Add a loaf of hot French bread to dip into the last bit of delicious sauce, and you have a comforting country-French dinner for family or friends. Serves 6-8.

3 lbs.	beef bottom round steak, cut into 1 1/4 inch (3 cm) cubes	1.5 kg
2	onions, coarsely chopped	2
2 tsp.	dried thyme	10 mL
1 tbsp.	cracked black peppercorns	15 mL
3 tbsp.	green peppercorns, drained	45 mL
3	bay leaves, crumbled	3
3 tbsp.	olive oil	45 mL
1/4 tsp.	ground cloves	1 mL
3 cups	red wine	750 mL
2 tbsp.	*each* butter and olive oil	30 mL
3 cups	carrots, peeled and sliced into rounds	750 mL
1	8 oz. (250 g) piece slab bacon, cut into 1/4 x 1 inch (6 mm x 2.5 cm) sticks	1
2 tsp.	sugar	10 mL
4 tbsp.	all-purpose flour	60 mL
	salt to taste	
1 cup	rich beef stock	250 mL
4 tbsp.	butter	60 mL
1 lb.	tiny white onions, peeled (about 3 cups (750 mL))	500 g
3/4 lb.	fresh mushrooms, tightly capped, wiped clean with a damp cloth (not washed), halved	375 g
4 tbsp.	finely minced fresh parsley	60 mL
	Buttery Croûtes (recipe follows)	

Marinate the beef cubes in a large bowl with the chopped onion, thyme, black pepper, green peppercorns, bay leaves, the 3 tbsp. (45 mL) olive oil, cloves, and red wine overnight, or 3 hours at room temperature.

To prepare the stew, heat the 2 tbsp. (30 mL) each butter and olive oil in a large, heavy Dutch oven or stainless steel pot over medium-high heat. Remove the beef from the marinade and pat dry. Add the beef to the pot and sauté, stirring, until lightly browned on all sides. Add the carrots and bacon and continue to sauté until lightly browned, adding the sugar during the last minute. Sprinkle the meat and vegetables with the flour and cook, stirring, until the mixture is a light brown, taking care not to scorch the flour. Stir in salt to taste.

Add the reserved marinade and beef stock, and bring the mixture to a simmer. Cover the pan tightly and simmer the stew over the lowest heat for 3 hours, or bake in a 300°F (150°C) oven for 3 hours. Stir the stew 2-3 times during cooking.

While the stew is simmering, melt 2 tbsp. (30 mL) of the butter, and sauté the tiny onions slowly until they carmelize and turn a rich golden brown on all sides. Heat the remaining 2 tbsp. (30 mL) butter and sauté the halved mushrooms until lightly golden on all sides.

Uncover the finished stew and stir in the onions and mushrooms. Heat the stew through for 15 minutes, uncovered, and taste and correct for seasonings. Set aside 30 minutes before serving.

Sprinkle the warm stew with the minced parsley. Tuck in the croûtes, and serve.

BUTTERY CROÛTES

8	slices firm white bread, at least 1/4 inch (6 mm) thick, crusts trimmed, cut in half diagonally to form triangles	8
4 tbsp.	butter	60 mL
4 tbsp.	olive oil	60 mL

Air-dry the bread triangles on a wire rack for several hours. Heat the butter and oil in a large non-stick skillet over medium heat. Fry the triangles, several at a time, until crispy and golden brown on both sides. Set aside on brown paper to cool. Serve within 2-3 hours.

ELGIAN BEEF AND ALE STEW

The Belgians have a favourite stew of braised beef with beer, sugary onions, and prunes. It is called Carbonnade Flamande, and anyone who has tasted this fabled dish has longed for more. The stew almost takes care of itself in the oven, and needs only some wide egg noodles and a loaf of rich peasant-style bread to complete the meal. Serve with tankards of cold apple cider. Serves 6.

2 tbsp.	vegetable oil	30 mL
2 tbsp.	bacon drippings	30 mL
4 tbsp.	flour	60 mL
2 tsp.	salt	10 mL
1 tsp.	black pepper	5 mL
1 tsp.	ground allspice	5 mL
3 lbs.	boneless beef chuck, cut into 1 inch (2.5 cm) cubes	1.5 kg
4	medium onions, halved and sliced	4
1	large clove garlic, crushed	1
2 tbsp.	brown sugar, packed	30 mL
2 tbsp.	red wine vinegar	30 mL
2 cups	dark beer or ale, or 12 oz. (375 mL) beer plus 1/4 cup (50 mL) water	500 mL
2	bay leaves	2
1	2 inch (5 cm) whole cinnamon stick	1
1 tsp.	*each* dried thyme, savoury, and marjoram	5 mL
15-18	plump dried prunes (not pitted)	15-18
1 lb.	egg noodles	500 g
2-3 tbsp.	softened butter	30-45 mL

Heat the vegetable oil and bacon drippings in a large, heavy Dutch oven over medium-high heat. In a large bowl whisk together the flour, salt, pepper, and allspice. Dredge the beef cubes in the flour mixture lightly to coat on all sides. Add the beef to the hot oil and brown quickly on all sides, tossing with a wooden spoon. With a slotted spoon, remove the beef to a platter and add the onions to the drippings in the pot. Quickly sauté the onions 3-4 minutes, stirring, until just slightly softened and pale golden on the edges. Add the garlic and brown sugar and sauté 1-2 minutes to flavour and carmelize slightly. Add the vinegar and cook over high heat 1-2 minutes until syrupy.

Stir in the beer, bay leaves, cinnamon stick, thyme, savoury, and marjoram. Gently bring the mixture to a boil. Return the browned beef to the pot, stir gently to combine the ingredients, and bring to a simmer.

Cover the pot and place it in a heated 325°F (160°C) oven. Bake the stew 1 hour, uncover, and add prunes. Bake, covered, 1 1/2-2 hours longer, removing the lid during the final 30 minutes to thicken sauce. Remove the stew from the oven and let stand 30 minutes before serving.

Cook the egg noodles according to package directions, tossing with the softened butter before serving alongside the warm stew.

OLD WORLD BEEF GOULASH WITH CARAWAY AND ONIONS

The most famous and beloved of all Hungarian dishes, goulash can be traced back hundreds of years. It warms the heart and appetite—just the thing to have simmering in the oven on a cold day. Chock full of savoury beef, and flavoured with paprika and caraway, this hearty stew needs only some wide egg noodles and a fresh, crisp cabbage salad as accompaniments. Serves 6.

4 tbsp.	vegetable oil or bacon drippings	60 mL
2	very large onions, halved and sliced	2
3	cloves garlic, slivered	3
2 tsp.	whole caraway seeds, slightly crushed	10 mL
2 tbsp.	paprika	30 mL
2 tbsp.	brown sugar, packed	30 mL
2 tbsp.	red wine vinegar	30 mL
1	5 1/2 oz. (156 mL) tin tomato paste	1
4 cups	rich beef stock or broth	1 L
3 lbs.	boneless beef chuck, cut into 1 1/2 inch (3.5 cm) cubes	1.5 kg
6 oz.	bacon or Gammon bacon, cut into 1/2 inch (1 cm) dice	175 mL
2 tsp.	salt	10 mL
dash	cayenne pepper	dash
1 tsp.	black pepper	5 mL
1 1/2 cups	sour cream	375 mL
4 tbsp.	all-purpose flour	60 mL
4 tbsp.	minced fresh parsley	60 mL

Heat the vegetable oil in a large, heavy Dutch oven or enameled cast-iron pot. Add the onions and sauté over medium-high heat 5-7 minutes until pale golden. Add the garlic, caraway seeds, paprika, and brown sugar, and sauté 3-4 minutes longer. Add the vinegar and heat 2-3 minutes to burn off the sharp flavour. Stir in the tomato paste and beef stock. Heat to a simmer. Set the pot aside to simmer over medium heat while browning the beef separately in another pan.

Heat the oven to 325°F (160°C). In a large, heavy skillet, sauté the bacon over medium-high heat, stirring, until softened and pale golden. Pat the beef cubes dry. In several batches, add the beef to the bacon and sauté quickly to brown on all sides, seasoning the meat as it browns with the salt, cayenne, and black pepper. When each batch is browned, transfer it to the simmering stew pot. After all the beef and bacon has been added to the stew pot, bring the mixture to a simmer. Cover and bake about 2 hours, or until the meat is very tender and the sauce is enriched.

Remove the pot from the oven, uncover, and skim excess fat from the surface. Whisk together the sour cream and flour until blended thoroughly and stir gently into the goulash. Simmer 5-7 minutes to thicken the sauce. Taste and correct for salt and pepper. Transfer the stew to a warmed tureen or large, deep crockery bowl. Sprinkle with minced parsley and serve.

Note: Goulash may be prepared a day ahead of time, up to the point of thickening with the sour cream-flour mixture. Chill, covered, overnight. Skim off any hardened fat. Heat over medium-low heat to simmering, and enrich with the sour cream-flour mixture before serving.

MIDDLE EASTERN SPICED LAMB

Here is a spicy, unusual stew: chunks of tender lamb and colourful vegetables bathed in the distinctive flavours of the Middle East. Serve it on a bed of rice studded with plump raisins and toasted slivered almonds. For an exotic touch, add a bit of turmeric to the rice-cooking water—it will turn a beautiful golden yellow. Serves 4-6.

2 tbsp.	olive oil	30 mL
2 lbs.	shoulder of lamb, trimmed, cut into 3/4 inch (2 cm) cubes	1 kg
1	medium onion, finely chopped	1
2	cloves garlic, crushed	2
6 tbsp.	tomato paste	90 mL
2	large tomatoes, peeled, seeded, and chopped	2
1	red bell pepper, sliced	1
1 tsp.	*each* cumin, coriander, and curry powder	5 mL
1/2 tsp.	*each* turmeric, ground ginger, and cinnamon	2 mL
pinch	cayenne pepper, or to taste	pinch
2	carrots, peeled and sliced	2
1	medium turnip, peeled and cubed (about 2 cups (500 mL))	1
1	zucchini, sliced	1
4 cups	peeled, cubed squash in 3/4 inch (2 cm) cubes	1 L
2 1/2-3 cups	cold water	625-750 mL
	salt and pepper to taste	
	sliced green onions and lemon wedges for garnish	

In a large saucepan, heat the oil. Add the meat, onion, and garlic and sauté over medium-high heat, stirring, until the meat loses its pink colour, about 4 minutes.

Add the tomato paste and cook, stirring, over medium heat for 2 minutes. Add the tomatoes, red pepper, cumin, coriander, curry, turmeric, ginger, cinnamon, and cayenne. Reduce the heat to low, cover the pan, and simmer 5 minutes. Stir in the carrots, turnip, zucchini, squash, and water. Cover the pan and simmer for 1 1/2-2 hours, stirring occasionally, until the meat is tender. Season to taste with salt and pepper.

Garnish with sliced green onions and lemon wedges, and serve.

DILLED LAMB STEW

The Greeks love lamb stew, and they have a palette of flavourings that is unrivalled. This simple stew is a delicate combination of lamb, lemon, dill, artichokes, and a delicious egg-lemon sauce. Serve with hot boiled orzo (rice-shaped pasta) or boiled potatoes, fresh green beans dressed with butter and garlic, and broiled fresh tomatoes. Serves 6.

3 tbsp.	olive oil	45 mL
3 lbs.	lamb riblets, cut into 2-bone sections	1.5 kg
	salt and freshly ground black pepper to taste	
1	large onion, halved and thinly sliced	1
2	large cloves garlic, slivered	2
3 cups	celery, cut crosswise into 1/2 inch (1 cm) pieces	750 mL
1 cup	*each* dry white wine and chicken stock	250 mL
2	14 oz. (398 mL) packages frozen artichoke hearts, thawed, or 2 14 oz. (398 mL) cans, drained	2
3 tbsp.	*each* finely minced fresh dill and parsley	45 mL
3	eggs	3
	juice of 2 lemons	
3 tbsp.	minced fresh parsley	45 mL
	sprigs of fresh dill for garnish	

Heat the olive oil in a very large stock pot over medium-high heat. Add the lamb riblets and quickly brown on all sides, stirring, and seasoning with salt and pepper. Remove the browned riblets and set aside. Add the onion, garlic, and celery to the drippings in the pot, and quickly sauté until slightly softened. Add the wine and stock, bring to a simmer, and return the browned lamb to the pot. Return the liquid to a simmer over medium heat, partially cover the pot, and simmer the stew 1 1/2 hours or until the meat is tender. Uncover and stir in the artichoke hearts and the 3 tbsp. (45 mL) each dill and parsley, and heat through for 10 minutes, uncovered. (The stew may be set aside for several hours at this point.)

Just before serving, prepare the thickening sauce. Whisk together the eggs and lemon juice in a bowl until light. Slowly add a ladleful or two of the warm stew liquid to the egg mixture, whisking as the liquid is added. Slowly pour this warmed mixture into the stew, and stir gently over the lowest heat 2-3 minutes until the sauce thickens, being careful not to curdle the sauce. Remove the hot stew from the heat, and allow it to rest 10-15 minutes before serving. The sauce will continue to thicken.

Sprinkle with the 3 tbsp. (45 mL) minced parsley and garnish with sprigs of fresh dill.

CAJUN CHICKEN GUMBO

This spicy, fragrant stew-like dish comes right from the heart of the French Quarter in New Orleans. Full of chicken and smoked sausage, it is great as the main event on a chilly evening. Serve it in big bowls, topped with a mound of white rice and a big bowl of Creole Green Sauce. Serves 6.

1	3 lb. (1.5 kg) frying chicken, cut into serving pieces (2 drumsticks, 2 thighs, 2 wings, 1 breast cut into 4 pieces)	1
2/3 cup	vegetable oil	150 mL
1/2 cup	all-purpose flour	125 mL
1 lb.	smoked sausage (Polish, garlic coil, or Mennonite), cut into 3/4 inch (2 cm) thick slices	500 g
1/2 lb.	baked ham, cut into 1/2 inch (1 cm) cubes	250 g
1	green bell pepper, diced	1
1	onion, coarsely diced	1
1 cup	sliced green onions (about 1 bunch)	250 mL
2	large cloves garlic, minced	2
1 cup	chopped celery (about 2 medium stalks)	250 mL
2 tbsp.	sugar	30 mL
1 tsp.	*each* salt, ground cloves, thyme, and cayenne	5 mL
3	bay leaves, crumbled	3
2 cups	coarsely chopped tomatoes (fresh or canned, drained; about 3 medium if fresh)	500 mL
2	10 oz. (315 g) pkgs. frozen okra, sliced into 1 inch (2.5 cm) rounds (or use fresh okra, sliced)	2
3 cups	chicken stock	750 mL
6 cups	cooked white fluffy rice	1.5 L
	Creole Green Sauce (recipe follows)	

Pat the chicken pieces dry. Heat the oil in a large, heavy pot (cast-iron is ideal) and brown the chicken quickly over medium-high heat. Remove the chicken pieces after browning and set aside. Prepare a roux by adding the flour to the oil and drippings in the pan. Cook the flour, whisking, to a rich, nutty, deep mahogany brown. Immediately add the sliced sausage, ham cubes, green pepper, onion, green onions, garlic, and celery to the hot roux. Cook, stirring, 12 minutes until tender.

Add the sugar, salt, cloves, thyme, cayenne, bay leaves, tomatoes, okra, and chicken stock. Heat until bubbly and add the browned chicken pieces. Simmer the gumbo 1 hour, or until the chicken is tender and the mixture is thickened to the consistency of a thin stew. Taste and correct for salt. Remove from the heat for 20 minutes (or cool, chill, and reheat before serving). Serve the gumbo in large bowls, topping each serving with 1 cup (250 mL) white rice. Pass a bowl of the chilled Creole Green Sauce.

CREOLE GREEN SAUCE

1	bunch green onions, thinly sliced	1
1 cup	finely minced fresh parsley	250 mL
1	large clove garlic, finely minced	1
2/3 cup	olive oil	150 mL
2 tbsp.	red wine vinegar	30 mL
pinch	sugar	pinch
1 tsp.	salt	5 mL
2 tbsp.	fresh lime juice	30 mL
6-8 drops	bottled hot pepper sauce	6-8 drops

Combine all ingredients in a bowl (a food processor is ideal, but not necessary). Whisk to a grainy-chunky salsa-like sauce. Chill several hours to blend the flavours. Serve cool or at room temperature.

OLD-FASHIONED CHICKEN STEW WITH DUMPLINGS

Who doesn't wax rhapsodic over memories of a big pot of savoury chicken stew with creamy gravy, topped with big, puffy, herb-flecked dumplings! On a cool evening, nothing beats this hearty dinner, perfect for the whole family, from kids to grandfolks. The secret to great dumplings? A light hand—and never, ever peek until the cooking time is up. Serve with leafy mixed fresh greens drizzled with a mustardy vinaigrette, and big glasses of ice cold milk. Then gather 'round the table for a great supper. Serves 6.

1	3 lb. (1.5 kg) frying chicken, cut up	1
2 tbsp.	butter	30 mL
4 oz.	slab bacon, cut into 1/2 inch (1 cm) dice	125 g
1	large onion, cut into 1 inch (2.5 cm) cubes	1
1 1/2 cups	*each* coarsely cubed (1 inch (2.5cm) cubes) peeled carrots, parsnips, rutabagas, and potatoes	375 mL
6 tbsp.	all-purpose flour	90 mL
3 cups	rich chicken stock	750 mL
1 cup	*each* milk and whipping cream	250 mL
1/2 cup	dry sherry	125 mL
1 tbsp.	finely grated lemon rind	15 mL
1 tsp.	*each* salt, cracked black pepper, and thyme	5 mL
2 tbsp.	fresh lemon juice	30 mL
1/4 tsp.	ground nutmeg	1 mL
	Savoury Sage Dumplings (recipe follows)	

Rinse the chicken pieces in cool water and pat completely dry. Heat the butter over medium-high heat in a large 5-6 quart (5-6 L) Dutch oven until bubbly, and add the chicken pieces. Brown quickly on all sides until pale golden. Remove the browned chicken to a platter and set aside.

In the remaining drippings, sauté the bacon and onions, stirring, until the onion is pale golden and the bacon is slightly crisped. Remove the mixture with a slotted spoon, add it to the chicken pieces, and set aside.

Blanch the vegetables in boiling salted water until barely tender. Drain.

Sprinkle the flour over the pan drippings, loosening up any bits clinging to bottom of the pan, and cook until bubbly, about 3 minutes. Whisk in the chicken stock and bring to a boil. Cook 2-3 minutes. Whisk in the milk, cream, sherry, lemon rind, salt, pepper, thyme, lemon juice, and nutmeg. Bring the mixture to a gentle boil, reduce the heat, and add the chicken, onions, bacon, and blanched vegetables.

Return the stew to a simmer, partially cover, and cook 30 minutes until the chicken is almost tender. Skim off any fat that rises to the surface. Prepare the dumpling mixture as the stew simmers.

SAVOURY SAGE DUMPLINGS

2 cups	all-purpose flour	500 mL
4 tsp.	baking powder	20 mL
1/2 tsp.	*each* salt and cracked black pepper	2 mL
3 tbsp.	minced fresh sage	45 mL
	or 1 tbsp. (15 mL) dried sage, crumbled	
2 tbsp.	minced fresh parsley	30 mL
1 tbsp.	finely grated lemon rind	15 mL
6 tbsp.	chilled butter	90 mL
1 cup	buttermilk	250 mL

Sift together the flour, baking powder, salt, and pepper. Whisk in the minced sage, parsley, and lemon rind. With a pastry blender, cut in the butter until the mixture resembles coarse crumbs. Add the buttermilk and stir lightly with a fork until the dough holds together and cleans the sides of the bowl. Gently form the dough into 12 rough-shaped balls, handling lightly with floured hands.

Drop the dumplings on the stew by large spoonfuls, leaving a bit of space between them for expanding. Cover the pot tightly with a domed lid and cook over low heat 20-25 minutes (do not peek!) until the dumplings are puffed, firm, and springy to the touch. They are done when a thin wooden skewer inserted in the centre comes out clean.

Serve the stew at once, piping hot, ladled into wide, shallow soup bowls with several dumplings in each bowl. Serve some of the rich gravy on the side.

SPICED CHICKEN STEW WITH APRICOTS

Here is a chicken stew with a difference: a touch of peanut butter and a bouquet of special spices, complemented by tangy lemon and sweet apricots. Serve it with hot steamed rice and tender-crisp green beans or broccoli. Serves 4.

2 tbsp.	margarine or butter	30 mL
1 tbsp.	vegetable oil	15 mL
2 lbs.	chicken pieces, skinned, cut in serving-size portions	1 kg
1	large onion, chopped	1
2	cloves garlic, crushed	2
1 1/2 tsp.	curry powder	7 mL
1/2 tsp.	*each* coriander and chili powder	2 mL
1 3/4 cups	chicken stock	425 mL
1/2 cup	chunky peanut butter	125 mL
1/2 cup	dried apricots, halved	125 mL
1/3 cup	dark raisins	75 mL
1 tbsp.	brown sugar	15 mL
1 tbsp.	lemon juice	15 mL
	salt to taste	
1/3 cup	roasted peanuts	75 mL

In a large saucepan, heat the margarine and oil. Add the chicken pieces and sauté 4-5 minutes, turning occasionally, until browned on all sides. Remove from the pan and set aside.

Drain off all but 2 tbsp. (30 mL) fat. Add the onion and garlic to the pan and sauté over medium heat for 3 minutes until soft. Stir in the curry powder, coriander, and chili powder and sauté 30 seconds, stirring. Pour in the chicken stock and peanut butter, stirring and scraping the bottom of the pan. Bring the mixture to a boil and stir in the apricots, raisins, brown sugar, and lemon juice. Return the chicken to the pan.

Reduce the heat to low, cover the pan, and simmer about 40 minutes or until the chicken is tender. Season with salt to taste. Place the stew in a warm serving dish and serve sprinkled with the peanuts.

Opposite: (top to bottom) Mariners' Stew (p. 115), Provençal Fish Fillets (p. 74).

FRESH VEGETABLE CURRY

Gently cooked with several piquant spices and a shot of mustard seeds, these familiar vegetables become food for the adventurous in this strong, hot, meatless curry. Plain yogurt and mango chutney are the perfect cooling accompaniments. Serves 4-6.

4 tbsp.	margarine or butter	60 mL
1	large onion, chopped	1
2	cloves garlic, crushed	2
1 tbsp.	very finely chopped fresh root ginger	15 mL
1 tsp.	mustard seeds	5 mL
3	large potatoes, peeled and cut into 1 inch (2.5 cm) chunks	3
3	large carrots, peeled and sliced	3
3	large tomatoes, coarsely chopped	3
2	zucchini, sliced 1/4 inch (6 mm) thick	2
4 oz.	green beans, trimmed and cut into 1 inch (2.5 cm) lengths	125 g
	juice of 1/2 lemon	
1 tbsp.	curry powder	15 mL
1 tsp.	coriander	5 mL
1 tsp.	turmeric	5 mL
1/2 tsp.	*each* chili powder, cumin powder, and salt	2 mL
1	bay leaf	1

Melt the margarine in a large saucepan. Add the onion, garlic, and ginger and sauté over medium heat for 3 minutes. Stir in the mustard seeds and sauté for 30 seconds. Add the potatoes, carrots, tomatoes, zucchini, beans, and lemon juice. Stir, cover, and cook over medium-low heat for 10 minutes, stirring occasionally.

Stir in the curry powder, coriander, turmeric, chili, cumin, salt, and bay leaf. Simmer, covered, 10 minutes. Pour in just enough water to make a thick, rich gravy, about 1/2 cup (125 mL). Cover and simmer 15 minutes longer or until the vegetables are cooked. Remove and discard the bay leaf. Serve hot.

PEASANT-STYLE COQ AU VIN WITH PARSLEYED CROUTONS

Coq au vin, a specialty of the Burgundy region of France, is a justly famous stew of plump chicken, bacon, onions, and fresh mushrooms in a sauce rich with red wine. Splurge on a good bottle of burgundy and serve this dish with pride to a group of special friends. Begin the meal with slices of a rich paté, follow with a crisp mixed green salad with an herb-flecked vinaigrette, and then bring on the stew—with a hot, crispy baguette or two to dip into the delicious sauce! Serves 4-6.

5 tbsp.	butter	75 mL
1	3 1/2 lb. (1.75 kg) frying chicken, cut up	1
	salt and freshly ground black pepper to taste	
6 oz.	slab bacon, cut into lardons	175 mL
	(thick matchsticks) 1/4 x 1 inch (6 mm x 2.5 cm)	
24	small boiling onions, peeled	24
3	large cloves garlic, slivered	3
4 tbsp.	brandy	60 mL
1 tbsp.	sugar	15 mL
1 tbsp.	red wine vinegar	15 mL
1 tbsp.	fresh thyme, *or*	15 mL
1 tsp.	dried thyme	5 mL
1	bay leaf	1
3 cups	burgundy wine	750 mL
3/4 lb.	fresh mushrooms, tightly capped and unblemished, wiped clean (do not wash)	375 g
3 tbsp.	*each* softened butter and all-purpose flour	45 mL
12	Parsleyed Croutons (recipe follows)	12
	minced fresh parsley	

Heat 2 tbsp. (30 mL) of the butter in a large pan over medium heat until bubbly. Pat the chicken pieces dry and brown in the hot butter, turning, until pale golden brown on all sides. Season the chicken lightly with salt and pepper as it browns. Remove the chicken to a platter and set aside.

Add the bacon lardons and boiling onions to the pan drippings and sauté 7-8 minutes until glossy and pale golden on all sides. Add the slivered garlic and sauté 1-2 minutes to flavour the mixture. Add the brandy, heat several seconds, and ignite. Allow the flames to die down, stir up all bits clinging to the pan, and cook until syrupy and glazed. Stir in the sugar and vinegar and cook until bubbly, about 1 minute. Add the thyme, bay leaf, and red wine. Bring the mixture to a simmer and return the chicken to the pot. Return to a simmer over medium heat, partially cover, and simmer 1 1/2 hours.

Meanwhile, heat the remaining 3 tbsp. (45 mL) butter in a skillet over medium-high heat, add the mushrooms, and quickly sauté, stirring, until golden brown on all sides. Uncover the stew and add the mushrooms. Stir to combine, and season with salt and pepper to taste. Simmer the stew, uncovered, 15 minutes.

Make a *beurre manié* by combining the softened butter and flour to a paste. Add it to the finished stew, a small amount at a time, to thicken the sauce. Taste and correct for seasonings. Remove the stew from the heat, and let stand 20 minutes before serving. Serve the Coq au Vin on rustic crockery plates, each garnished with several Parsleyed Croutons tucked onto the sides of the plate. Garnish each serving with a sprinkling of minced parsley.

PARSLEYED CROUTONS

12	1/2 inch (1 cm) thick slices firm white bread	12
	3 inch (7.5 cm) heart-shaped cookie cutter	
6 tbsp.	butter	90 mL
2 tbsp.	olive oil	30 mL
	garlic seasoning salt to taste	
1/2 cup	finely minced fresh parsley	125 mL

Cut a heart from the centre of each slice bread with cookie cutter and air-dry the croutons several hours. Heat the butter and olive oil in a large non-stick skillet over medium-high heat until bubbly. Fry the croutons to a golden brown on each side, seasoning with garlic seasoning salt during the final minute. Transfer the hot croutons to a sheet of brown paper and sprinkle at once with the minced parsley. Set aside to cool.

APLE SYRUP BAKED BEANS

On a cold, blustery night, nothing beats the east coast tradition of a plate of hot baked beans—rich with the flavours of maple syrup, onions, mustard, and smoked pork. This recipe is sure to warm the tummies and hearts of all who dip into the bean pot. Serve with hot grilled smoked sausages, a crisp cabbage salad, buttered slices of brown bread, and a crock of grainy mustard. Terrific the day you bake them, even better the next day. Serves 6-8.

1 lb.	(2 1/2 cups (625 mL)) dried navy or white beans, soaked in cold water overnight and drained	500 g
6 tbsp.	brown sugar, packed	90 mL
2/3 cup	dark maple syrup	150 mL
1 tbsp.	dry English-style mustard	15 mL
1/2 tsp.	*each* ground allspice and ginger	2 mL
2 tsp.	salt	10 mL
1/2 tsp.	cracked black pepper	2 mL
1	medium onion, diced	1
1	smoked ham hock, cracked in several places	1
1	6 oz. (180 g) piece salt pork, cut into 3 pieces, each scored in a checkerboard pattern	1

Place the drained, soaked beans into a saucepan and cover with cold water. Bring to a boil, remove the pan from the heat, and let stand 1 hour. Drain the beans, reserving the water. Transfer the beans to a bean pot with a tight-fitting lid (a crockery pot is best). Stir in the brown sugar, maple syrup, mustard, allspice, ginger, salt, pepper, and onion. Bury the cracked ham hock in the centre of the pot, along with 2 of the pieces of salt pork. Place the remaining piece of salt pork on top of the beans. Add enough of the reserved water to just cover the beans. Cover the pot and bake the beans in a heated 275°F (140°C) oven 5-7 hours.

Check the beans every 2 hours, making sure they are still moist. Add a little water if needed. Uncover the pot during the final hour to brown the top piece of pork and thicken the juices. Remove the beans from the oven when they are tender, glossy, syrupy, and richly browned. Allow to cool 1-2 hours before serving.

When serving, make sure that each portion contains a bit of the smoked ham hock and some of the crisp salt pork.

ISHERMAN'S STEW

The tang of fresh orange, blended with classic go-togethers tomato and fragrant basil, makes the delicious difference in this hearty fish stew. With the year-round abundant supply of fresh fish in the seafood department, you can change the fish with the season. Serve this as a satisfying lunch or light supper with warm bagels, croissants, or cheese rolls. Serves 4-6.

2 tbsp.	olive oil	30 mL
1	medium onion, finely chopped	1
1	large leek, sliced	1
2	large cloves garlic, crushed	2
1 tsp.	paprika	5 mL
1	28 oz. (796 mL) can tomatoes	1
1 tsp.	sugar	5 mL
2	medium potatoes, peeled and diced	2
1	large carrot, peeled and sliced	1
1/2	green bell pepper, diced	1/2
1	bay leaf	1
3 tbsp.	fresh orange juice	45 mL
1 tsp.	grated orange rind	5 mL
2 cups	water	500 mL
1 lb.	red snapper, cod, or halibut, skinned, boned, and cut into strips	500 g
1 1/2 cups	finely chopped broccoli florets	375 mL
2 tbsp.	chopped fresh basil	30 mL
	salt and pepper to taste	
1 cup	grated Swiss cheese	250 mL

Heat the oil in a large saucepan. Add the onion, leek, and garlic and sauté 2-3 minutes until soft but not brown. Stir in the paprika and sauté 30 seconds. Add the tomatoes and sugar and crush the tomatoes in the pan with a wooden spoon. Stir in the potatoes, carrot, green pepper, bay leaf, orange juice, orange rind, and water. Bring to a boil, cover, and simmer 15 minutes. Add the fish and broccoli and simmer 5-8 minutes, until both are cooked. (The fish will be white and opaque.) Remove and discard the bay leaf. Stir in the basil and season to taste with salt and pepper. Sprinkle with cheese and serve.

SEAFOOD STEW WITH SAFFRON

Luscious seafood—available all year round—and a hint of saffron make this stew special. Add a crisp green salad and warm dinner rolls and get ready for a memorable dinner! Serves 4.

16	prawns	16
3 cups	chicken stock or canned broth	750 mL
1	small red bell pepper	1
4 tbsp.	olive oil	60 mL
1 lb.	whitefish steaks (halibut, cod, or your favourite similar fish), boned and cut into 1 inch (2.5 cm) pieces	500 g
1/2 lb.	squid, cleaned and cut into 1/4 inch (6 mm) rings (about 6 squid)	250 g
1	medium onion, chopped	1
2	cloves garlic, chopped	2
2	tomatoes, chopped	2
3/4 cup	short grain rice	175 mL
2	pinches saffron threads or powder	2
1 cup	frozen peas	250 mL
	chopped parsley and lemon wedges for garnish	

Shell the prawns and set aside. Boil the shells in the chicken stock for 10 minutes. Strain the liquid into a measuring cup, pressing the shells to extract all the liquid. Discard the shells. Add more chicken stock or water to make 3 cups (750 mL). Char the red pepper on a foil-lined baking sheet under the broiler, turning, until all sides are blackened. Place it in a paper bag for a few minutes. Under running water, remove the skin and seeds. Cut into strips and set aside.

Heat 2 tbsp. (30 mL) of the oil in a paella pan or stove-top-to-oven casserole. Over medium heat, sauté the white fish for 1 minute on each side. Remove to a platter. Repeat for the prawns and squid.

Add the remaining oil to the pan and over medium-low heat, sauté the onions until limp. Add the garlic and cook for 1 minute. Add the tomatoes and rice, and over medium-high heat, cook until the rice is lightly browned.

Dissolve the saffron in the reserved chicken broth and pour over the rice mixture. Boil, uncovered, for 10 minutes, stirring occasionally or until the rice is no longer soupy and some liquid remains.

Heat the oven to 350°F (180°C). Stir in the pepper and seafood, pushing them into the hot rice. Bake 15-20 minutes or until the liquid is absorbed. Remove the casserole from the oven and stir in the peas. Let stand 10 minutes before serving. Garnish with parsley and lemon.

Mariners' Stew

This is a hearty seafood stew, best served with large chunks of crusty baguette for dipping into the delicious sauce. Accompany it with a chilled salad of mixed citrus fruit in a honey-lime dressing. Serves 4-6.

1	large onion, chopped	1
2 tbsp.	butter	30 mL
1 tbsp.	all-purpose flour	15 mL
2 tsp.	salt	10 mL
1 tsp.	white pepper	5 mL
4 tbsp.	chopped fresh parsley	60 mL
1 tsp.	dried oregano	5 mL
1	28 oz. (796 mL) can stewed tomatoes	1
1	small fresh ginger root, peeled	1
2 lbs.	snapper, haddock, cod, or halibut, cut into 1 inch (2.5 cm) cubes	1 kg
2	eggs	2
2 tbsp.	lemon or lime juice	30 mL
	chopped fresh parsley for garnish	

In a large microproof casserole, place the onion and butter. Cover and microwave on HIGH 100% power 2-4 minutes until the onion is soft. Blend in the flour, salt, pepper, and herbs. Stir in the tomatoes and ginger root. Cover and microwave on HIGH 100% power 3-5 minutes to bring to a boil. Reduce the power level to MEDIUM LOW 30% power and simmer 10 minutes. Add the fish, cover and microwave on HIGH 100% power 5-8 minutes until the fish is cooked. Remove and discard ginger root. Beat the eggs with the lemon juice.Stir into the stew, cover, and microwave on MEDIUM 50% power 2-3 minutes until slightly thickened. Serve hot in deep soup bowls, garnished with fresh parsley.

The Easy Gourmet features a photograph of this recipe on page 107.

SOUPS

Soup is a thoroughly versatile food—it can be a light lunch, a perfect first course at dinner, or the main event itself. Old-Fashioned Beef Stock and Old-Fashioned Chicken Stock are the start of simmered specialties like Italian Minestrone and Portuguese Caldo Gallego, or try the more unusual Smoked Cod and Corn Chowder or Cream of Chestnut and Mushroom Soup.

LD-FASHIONED BEEF STOCK

Making your own rich beef stock from scratch is simple and satisfying, and makes for great homemade soups and stews. This recipe yields about 4 quarts (4 L) of rich, beefy stock. Keep it in the fridge and use it within 3-4 days, or freeze it in 1 pint (500 mL) containers.

4 lbs.	assorted beef bones	2 kg
	(shanks, marrow bones, short ribs, shinbones)	
4 lbs.	veal bones, cracked	2 kg
	(shanks and shins are excellent)	
2	large onions, halved (skin on)	2
1	whole head garlic, halved horizontally	1
	(peel, root-end, and all)	
6	large carrots, rinsed and cut into 3 inch (7.5 cm) chunks	6
3	parsnips, rinsed and cut into 3 inch (7.5 cm) chunks	3
4	bay leaves	4
1	bunch fresh thyme	1
1	bunch fresh parsley	1
2	leeks, rinsed well and cut into 4 inch (10 cm) chunks	2
4	stalks celery, leaves attached, rinsed and cut into 4 inch (10 cm) chunks	4
4 tbsp.	vegetable oil	60 mL
1 tbsp.	whole black peppercorns	15 mL
8	whole cloves	8
1-2 tsp.	salt	5-10 mL
6-8 quarts	cold water	6-8 L

Place the beef bones, veal bones, onion, garlic, carrots, parsnips, bay leaves, thyme, parsley, leeks, and celery in a very large, heavy roasting pan. Drizzle all ingredients with the oil and toss lightly to coat. Place the pan in the lower third of a heated 375°F (190°C) oven. Roast the bones and vegetables 1 1/2 hours or until they are a rich golden brown. Remove from the oven.

Transfer all bones and vegetables and all drippings to a very large stock pot. Add the peppercorns, cloves, and salt. Cover with 6-8 quarts (6-8 L) cold water. Bring the liquid to a gentle boil, skimming off any foam as it rises to the surface. Reduce the heat to low and simmer the stock 5-6 hours. Turn the heat off, and cool the stock completely.

Strain the stock, discarding all bones and vegetables. Wash the stock pot completely and wipe dry. Return the strained stock to the pot, cover and refrigerate overnight. Lift off the hardened surface fat 24 hours later and discard. Freeze the finished stock in 1 pint (500 mL) containers for up to 6 months.

OLD-FASHIONED CHICKEN STOCK

Almost nothing beats a rich, old-fashioned, "like Grandma used to make" chicken stock, and having a stash on hand in the freezer insures that sumptuous soups, stews, risottos, and sauces can be prepared on short notice. Make sure to use a stewing chicken, not a fryer—the more mature the bird, the richer the end stock! Use the stock within 2-3 days, or keep it frozen in 1 pint (500 mL) containers. Makes about 4 quarts (4 L).

1	5-6 lb. (2.5-3 kg) stewing or boiling chicken	1
2 lbs.	chicken backs	1 kg
6 quarts	cold water	6 L
1	large onion, including skin,	1
	cut in half and studded with 8 whole cloves	
1	whole head garlic (peel, root-end, and all),	1
	halved horizontally	1
3	large carrots, rinsed and cut into 4 inch (10 cm) pieces	3
4	stalks celery (leaves included), rinsed and	4
	cut into 4 inch (10 cm) pieces	
1 bunch	fresh parsley, tied with string	1 bunch
1 bunch	fresh thyme, tied with string	1 bunch
2	bay leaves	2
2 tsp.	salt	10 mL
12	whole black peppercorns	12

Place the chicken and backs in a very large stock pot. Cover with 6 quarts (6 L) cold water. Bring to a gentle boil, skimming off any foam as it rises to the top. Simmer 30 minutes and skim again. Add the onion, garlic, carrots, celery, parsley, thyme, bay leaves, salt and peppercorns. Bring the liquid to a simmer. Reduce the heat to low, and simmer the stock 4 hours. Turn off the heat and allow the stock to cool completely.

Strain the stock, removing all solid ingredients. Wash the stock pot thoroughly and wipe dry. Return the strained stock to the pot, cover, and refrigerate 24 hours.

Spoon off the hardened surface fat and discard. Freeze the finished stock, which will be quite gelatinous and rich, in 1 pint (500 mL) containers for up to 6 months.

CALDO GALLEGO

Portugal gives us this hearty, lovely green soup, packed with potatoes, vitamin-rich kale, and smoked garlic sausage. Quickly made, this savoury soup makes a complete meal when accompanied by a basket of hot corn bread, fresh butter, and a delicious crème caramel for dessert. Serves 6.

6 tbsp.	olive oil	90 mL
1	large onion, diced	1
2-3	large cloves garlic, slivered	2-3
6	large boiling potatoes, peeled and coarsely cubed	6
2 quarts	beef stock or chicken stock	2 L
1 lb.	dry garlic-flavoured sausage (linguiça, garlic coil, chorizo, or pepperoni), sliced into 1/2 inch (1 cm) thick rounds	500 g
3-4 dashes	bottled hot pepper sauce	3-4 dashes
1-2 tbsp.	sherry wine vinegar	15-30 mL
1 lb.	kale, washed, drained, stacked, and cut into 1/2 inch (1 cm) wide ribbons	500 g
	salt and freshly ground black pepper to taste	
	extra-virgin olive oil	

Heat the olive oil in a large stock pot over medium-high heat. Add the onion and garlic and sauté, stirring, until pale golden. Add the potatoes and sauté 4-5 minutes until slightly golden in colour. Add the stock, bring to a simmer, partially cover the pot, and simmer 30 minutes, or until the potatoes are tender.

Add the sliced sausage, hot pepper sauce, and sherry wine vinegar. Heat, partially covered, 10 minutes. Uncover the soup and add the sliced kale. Simmer, uncovered, 15 minutes. Taste and correct for salt and pepper. Turn off the heat and let the soup rest 1-3 hours before serving for the best flavour.

Serve the soup in shallow bowls, each portion drizzled with olive oil and dusted with a grind of pepper.

BEST-EVER BEET BORSCHT

Borscht is a great soup to have on hand—simply wonderful served hot on a wintery night, with a dollop of sour cream and thick slices of fresh rye bread and butter. It is equally good served lukewarm, and it is the best several days after it is prepared. This recipe will make converts of anyone ambivalent about that earthy vegetable, the beet. Serves 8.

2 tbsp.	*each* butter and vegetable oil	30 mL
1	large onion, diced	1
2	cloves garlic, crushed	2
2 tbsp.	brown sugar, packed	30 mL
1 lb.	fresh beets (weighed without tops), peeled and cut into matchstick julienne (1/4 x 1 inch (6 mm x 2.5 cm))	500 g
2 cups	*each* julienned celery root and parsnips	500 g
1/4 cup	red wine vinegar or cider vinegar	60 mL
1	28 oz. (796 mL) can whole tomatoes, broken up, including juice	1
2 tsp.	salt	10 mL
1 tsp.	coarsely ground black pepper	5 mL
8 cups	beef broth	2 L
1	1 lb. (500 g) head cabbage, halved, cored and coarsely shredded	1
1 lb.	smoked Ukrainian or Mennonite sausage, sliced into 1/4 inch (6 mm) rounds	500 g
1/3 cup	minced fresh parsley	75 mL
1/3 cup	minced fresh dill	75 mL
2 cups	sour cream	500 mL

Heat the butter and oil in a large, deep stock pot over medium-high heat until bubbly. Add the onions and garlic, and quickly sauté until softened and lightly golden on the edges. Add the brown sugar, julienned beets, celery root, parsnips, and vinegar, and cook, stirring, 5 minutes. Add the tomatoes and their juice, salt, pepper, and beef broth, and bring to a simmer. Partially cover the pot and simmer about 1 hour.

Add the shredded cabbage and cook the soup 30 minutes. Add the sliced smoked sausage, stir, and simmer 15 minutes. Taste the soup and correct for salt. Finally, stir in the minced parsley and dill. Partially cover the soup and set aside 1-2 hours before serving.

Ladle soup into wide, shallow soup bowls. Top each serving with a generous dollop of sour cream.

The Easy Gourmet features a photograph of this recipe on page 125.

CHOCK FULL OF BEEF AND BARLEY SOUP POT

This soup is so satisfying and hearty that a loaf of crusty bread and a leafy endive salad is all you'll need to complete the menu. Loaded with chunky beef short ribs, barley, and seasonal root vegetables, it is the definitive stick-to-the-ribs soup! Serves 6-8.

4 lbs.	lean, meaty beef short ribs, cross cut into 2 inch (5 cm) pieces	2 kg
3 quarts	cold water	3 L
2	large onions, halved and thinly sliced	2
2	large cloves garlic, slivered	2
1	large celeriac (celery root), peeled and diced	1
2 cups	*each* coarsely diced parsnips, carrots, and celery (about 3 of each)	500 mL
2	leeks, sliced into thin rounds (white and tender green part only)	2
1 1/2 cups	pearl barley	375 mL
1	28 oz. (796 mL) can whole tomatoes, including liquid	1
2 tsp.	*each* dried thyme and cracked black pepper	10 mL
1 tbsp.	salt	15 mL
1/3 cup	fresh lemon juice	75 mL
	grated rind of 1 lemon	
1/3 cup	minced fresh parsley	75 mL

Rinse the short ribs under cold water and place in a large stock pot with the water. Bring to a simmer over medium heat. With a mesh strainer, skim off any foam as it rises to the surface. Simmer the ribs, partially covered, 1 1/2 hours. Set aside.

Strain the stock into a clean pot. Return the stock to a simmer, adding the onions, garlic, celeriac, parsnips, carrots, celery, and leeks. Slip the bones out of the ribs and cut the meat into 3/4 inch (2 cm) cubes. Return the meat to the soup. Simmer 1 1/2 hours. Rinse the barley under cold water and add it to the soup. Add the canned tomatoes with their juice, breaking up the tomatoes into coarse dice. Season with thyme, black pepper, and salt. Simmer 1 hour longer, or until the barley is very tender and the soup has thickened. Add water if the soup is too thick.

Add the lemon juice and rind, and simmer 30 minutes longer. Taste and correct for seasonings, adding additional lemon juice if needed. Stir in the parsley immediately before serving.

 AVOURITE SCOTCH BROTH

A traditional Scottish soup, this filling dish is a tasty, nutritious meal in itself—just add some warm whole-wheat dinner rolls and a crock of butter. For maximum flavour, refrigerate the broth overnight, and finish preparing the soup before serving. Serves 6-8.

2 lbs.	neck or shank of lamb, cut in pieces, trimmed	1 kg
8 cups	cold water	2 L
4 tbsp.	pearl barley	60 mL
4 tbsp.	dried yellow split peas	60 mL
1/2 tsp.	salt	2 mL
1/4 tsp.	pepper	1 mL
2	*each* medium leeks and carrots, sliced	2
1	large onion, chopped	1
1 1/2 cups	diced rutabaga	375 mL
4 cups	thin sliced cabbage	1 L
1 cup	frozen peas	250 mL

Place the meat in a large saucepan with the water, barley, split peas, salt, and pepper. Bring to a boil, cover, and simmer 1 1/2 hours until the meat is tender. (If you are preparing the soup ahead, refrigerate the broth overnight at this point.)

Lift the lamb from the pan and remove the meat from the bones. Discard the bones and cut the meat into small pieces. Set aside. Allow the mixture in the pan to cool slightly, unless refrigerated overnight. Skim off any fat.

Add the leeks, carrots, onion, and rutabaga to the pan. Bring to a boil, cover, and simmer 20 minutes. Add the cabbage and peas, and simmer 10 minutes longer, until all vegetables are cooked. Return the lamb to the pan, heat through, taste and correct for seasoning, and serve.

HERBED HAM AND RED LENTIL SOUP

Simple soups are often the best ones. The rich, meaty taste of a ham hock slowly simmered with vegetables and herbs gives this soup a hearty, satisfying flavour. Thick, chunky, and full-flavoured, this one goes well with a country-style whole-grain bread. Serves 4.

1	1 1/2 lb. (750 g) smoked ham hock	1
9 cups	cold water	2.25 L
1	large onion, chopped	1
2	large carrots, peeled and sliced	2
1	stalk celery, sliced (optional)	1
1 tsp.	dried mixed herbs	5 mL
1	bay leaf	1
1 cup	red lentils	250 mL
	salt and pepper to taste	

Place the ham hock in a large saucepan. Pour in cold water until the meat is almost covered. Add the onion, carrot, celery, herbs, and bay leaf. Bring to a boil, then cover and simmer 1 1/2 hours. Remove from heat and allow it to cool. (This can be done overnight in the refrigerator.) Skim off any fat from the surface.

Remove the hock from the soup. Cut off the outer skin and any fat and discard. Remove the meat from the bone and cut it into small pieces. Set the meat aside.

Return the stock to a boil. Add the lentils, reduce the heat to medium-low, and simmer, covered, 15-20 minutes or until the lentils are cooked. Remove and discard the bay leaf. Purée the soup in batches in a food processor or blender. Return the soup to the saucepan, add the ham, and reheat. The soup should be thick, but it can be thinned with a little water if necessary. Season to taste with salt and pepper, and serve.

Opposite: Best-Ever Beet Borscht (p. 120), Irish Whole Wheat Soda Bread (p. 151).

C REAMY CHUNKY CHICKEN SOUP

A delicate pale green with chunks of creamy white chicken meat, this soup is as good to look at as to eat. It is almost a meal in itself—just add a platter of crisp fresh vegetables and a basket of whole-grain bread. The recipe doubles well and freezes beautifully. Serves 4-5.

1 1/2 lbs.	chicken pieces, skinned	750 g
1	small onion, quartered	1
2	stalks celery, quartered	2
2	whole cloves	2
2	whole carrots, quartered	2
1	bay leaf	1
3 cups	coarsely chopped leeks (about 5), white and light green parts only	750 mL
1	medium potato, peeled and sliced	1
2 tbsp.	olive oil or water	30 mL
	salt, pepper, and nutmeg to taste	
2 tbsp.	whipping cream	30 mL
	chopped fresh parsley or chives for garnish	

Place the chicken, onion, celery, cloves, carrots, and bay leaf in a large pot. Cover with cold water and bring to a boil. Skim off any foam. Reduce the heat to a simmer and cook until the chicken is tender, about 20 minutes.

Remove the chicken and let it cool slightly, keeping the stock simmering on the stove. Strip the meat from the bones and return the bones to the simmering stock. Cut the meat into 1 inch (2.5 cm) pieces and set aside.

Place the leeks and potato in a large saucepan with the 2 tbsp. (30 mL) oil or water. Cover and steam over medium heat 5-10 minutes until tender.

Strain the stock, discarding the vegetables and bones. Add 2 cups (500 mL) of the stock to the leeks and potatoes, and cook until the vegetables are very soft. Cool slightly. Purée the vegetables and stock in a blender or food processor until very smooth. Return to a clean saucepan and add the chicken and 1 cup (250 mL) of the remaining stock. Stir well. Season to taste.

Just before serving, swirl in the whipping cream. Ladle the soup into warmed bowls and garnish with parsley or chives.

HEARTY SMOKED HAM AND PEA SOUP

Savoury, satisfying, nourishing, this homemade pea soup is chock full of smoked ham, celery, carrots, and fragrant herbs. Serve piping hot in big, wide soup bowls and top each serving with a generous handful of crispy celery-flavoured croutons. Add a great loaf of hearty whole-grain or rye bread, heated in the oven, and tankards of apple cider. Serves 6.

2 1/2 lbs.	smoked ham hocks (about 4)	1.25 kg
3 quarts	cold water	3 L
1 lb.	green split peas, rinsed in cold water and drained	500 g
3 tbsp.	butter	45 mL
1	large onion, diced	1
3	large carrots, peeled and diced	3
1/2 tsp.	*each* ground cloves and nutmeg	2 mL
2 tsp.	dried marjoram	10 mL
2 tsp.	sugar	10 mL
2 tsp.	whole celery seed	10 mL
	grated rind of 1 lemon	
1-2 tsp.	salt, or to taste	5-10 mL
1 tsp.	coarsely cracked black pepper	5 mL
2 cups	Crispy Celery Seed Croutons (recipe follows)	500 mL

Bring the ham hocks and cold water to a simmer in a large, deep stock pot. Partially cover the pot and simmer 2 1/2 hours. Remove the ham hocks from the stock and set aside to cool. (At this point, the stock may be cooled and refrigerated overnight so that the fat may be lifted off the surface before the soup is finished.) Skim off fat and scum.

Add the split peas to the stock, and simmer 2 hours. Heat the butter in a large non-stick skillet over medium heat until bubbly. Add the onion and carrots, and sauté, stirring, until softened and slightly golden. Add the cloves, nutmeg, marjoram, sugar, and celery seed, and heat 1-2 minutes to flavour the vegetables. Scrape the entire mixture into a soup pot and simmer 1 hour longer. Add 1 cup (250 mL) water if the soup is too thick.

While the soup is simmering, remove the meat from the cooled ham hocks, discarding the heavy rind and bones. Cut the meat into large chunks. Add the meat to the soup along with the lemon rind, salt, and generous grindings of black pepper. Heat the soup to piping hot, ladle into warmed soup bowls, and serve. Top each serving with a handful of Crispy Celery Seed Croutons.

CRISPY CELERY SEED CROUTONS

6 tbsp.	butter	90 mL
2 cups	diced whole-grain or whole wheat bread, air-dried several hours to firm	500 mL
2 tsp.	whole celery seeds, crushed	10 mL
	ground nutmeg to taste	
	garlic seasoning salt to taste	
	freshly ground black pepper to taste	

Heat the butter over medium heat in a large non-stick skillet until foaming. Add the bread cubes all at once and stir-fry quickly to coat in butter. Fry, stirring, until golden brown and crispy, about 5 minutes. During the final minute, season with celery seeds, and sprinkle evenly and lightly with nutmeg, garlic salt, and black pepper. Set the skillet aside to cool for several hours before serving. These croutons are best served freshly prepared.

CHUNKY SEAFOOD CHOWDER WITH HERBS

No one can resist a steaming bowl of thick seafood chowder on a cool evening. And with Canada's year-round, coast to coast bounty of fresh fish, this one is a snap to prepare. Serves 4-6.

6	slices bacon, diced	6
2 tbsp.	butter	30 mL
2 cups	sliced leeks, white and tender green part only (about 3 medium)	500 mL
6 cups	rich fish stock (or a mixture of bottled clam juice and chicken stock)	1.5 L
6 cups	peeled and cubed potatoes, soaked in cold water (about 6 large)	1.5 L
1 lb.	fresh salmon fillets, cut into 1 inch (2.5 cm) cubes	500 g
1 lb.	fresh cod, cut into 1 inch (2.5 cm) cubes	500 g
1 pint	shucked clams, drained	500 mL
2 cups	peeled, coarsely cubed Roma tomatoes	500 mL
2 tbsp.	tomato paste	30 mL
1 tsp.	sugar	5 mL
2 cups	whipping cream	500 mL
1/2 cup	dry white wine or vermouth	125 mL
2 tbsp.	fresh lemon juice	30 mL
1/3 cup	snipped fresh dill	75 mL
3 tbsp.	minced fresh parsley	45 mL
	salt and freshly ground black pepper to taste	

In a large stock pot, sauté the bacon and butter over medium-high heat until translucent and just pale golden. Add the sliced leeks, and sauté with the bacon until just softened, stirring. Add the fish stock and bring to a boil. Drain the potatoes and add to the stock. Reduce the heat to a simmer, partially cover the pot, and simmer about 25 minutes or until the potatoes are tender.

Stir in the cubed salmon, cod, clams, tomatoes, tomato paste, sugar, cream, and wine. Gently bring to a simmer, and cook uncovered 15 minutes until the liquid is bubbly and the fish is opaque and just firmed. Stir in the lemon juice, dill, parsley, salt, and pepper. Heat 10 minutes longer. Taste and correct for salt and pepper.

Allow the finished chowder to stand 30 minutes before serving in deep, wide soup bowls. Pass the pepper grinder!

SMOKED COD AND CORN CHOWDER

Chowders—rich, hearty, and nutritious—are true North American cuisine. Smoked cod gives an aromatic touch to this one, a thick, creamy, thoroughly irresistible chowder. Accompany it with a salad of mixed fresh greens and hot dinner rolls. Serves 4.

2 tbsp.	margarine or butter	30 mL
1	medium onion, finely chopped	1
2	medium potatoes, peeled and cut into small cubes (about 2 cups (500 mL))	2
1/2	medium green bell pepper, cut into small cubes	1/2
2 tbsp.	all-purpose flour	30 mL
3 cups	milk	750 mL
1/2 lb.	smoked cod	250 g
1	7 oz. (200 mL) can whole kernel corn, drained	1
1 tbsp.	chopped fresh parsley	15 mL
	salt and pepper to taste	

Melt the margarine in a medium saucepan. Add the onion and sauté over medium heat until soft but not brown, about 2-3 minutes. Add the potatoes and pepper and sauté 3 minutes, stirring occasionally. Add the flour and cook 30 seconds, stirring. Gradually pour in the milk, stirring. Bring the mixture to a boil, stirring until slightly thickened, then reduce the heat to low and simmer, covered, for 15 minutes or until the potatoes are cooked, stirring occasionally.

Meanwhile, place the cod in a skillet and cover with water. Bring to a boil, then reduce the heat and simmer, covered, about 10 minutes, until the fish is cooked. Skin, bone, and flake the fish and add it to the chowder with the corn. Heat through, stir in the chopped parsley, season to taste with salt and pepper, and serve.

EDITERRANEAN TOMATO FISH SOUP

This thick, tomato-based soup can be prepared ahead, for it reheats beautifully. It is almost a meal in itself—just add cheese-topped toasted French bread and you have a perfect winter's night dinner! Serves 4-6.

8 oz.	*each* cod, halibut, and snapper fillets	250 g
1	large onion, chopped	1
1	clove garlic, crushed	1
6 tbsp.	olive oil	90 mL
1	14 oz. (398 mL) can stewed tomatoes	1
2 tbsp.	tomato paste	30 mL
2 tbsp.	chopped fresh parsley	30 mL
4 cups	fish stock or water	1 L
1/2 cup	dry white wine (optional)	125 mL
1	bay leaf	1
1/2	lemon	1/2
	salt and freshly ground black pepper to taste	
1/2 cup	whipping cream	125 mL
	chopped fresh parsley for garnish	

Remove the skin and bones from the fish and cut each fillet into 1 inch (2.5 cm) pieces. Set aside.

Place the onion, garlic, and olive oil in a 12 cup (3 L) microproof casserole dish. Cover and microwave on HIGH 100% power 3-5 minutes until the onion is soft, stirring once during the cooking time.

Add stewed tomatoes, tomato paste and 2 tbsp. (30 mL) chopped parsley. Cover and microwave on MEDIUM 50% power 15 minutes. Add the prepared fish, fish stock or water, wine, bay leaf, and lemon. Cover and microwave on MEDIUM 50% power 30 minutes. Discard the bay leaf and lemon. Allow to cool slightly.

Remove 1 piece of fish for each serving. Purée the soup until smooth. Season to taste with salt and pepper. Blend in the cream, cover, and microwave on MEDIUM 50% power to reheat. Reduce the power level to MEDIUM LOW 30%, if necessary, to prevent boiling.

To serve, place one piece of reserved fish in each soup bowl, cover with soup, and garnish with chopped parsley.

I TALIAN MINESTRONE

Tomatoes, squashes, celery, onions, and tiny shell macaroni team up with classic Italian seasonings in this dish, called "Minestra" in Italy. The soup has a richly flavoured tomato base and the vegetables can vary with the season—try your favourites. Serve with robust bread or rolls. Makes 8 cups (2 L).

2 tbsp.	olive oil	30 mL
2 tbsp.	butter	30 mL
1	medium onion, chopped	1
2	leeks, white part only, coarsely chopped	2
2	cloves garlic, chopped	2
4	tomatoes, seeded and coarsely chopped	4
2 tbsp.	tomato paste	30 mL
2	carrots, peeled and coarsely chopped	2
2	stalks celery, peeled and coarsely chopped	2
2 cups	peeled and diced squash	500 mL
	(about 9 oz. (300 g))	
3 tbsp.	chopped fresh parsley	45 mL
1 tsp.	dried oregano	5 mL
1 tsp.	dried basil	5 mL
pinch	cayenne pepper	pinch
	freshly ground black pepper to taste	
1 cup	dried baby macaroni shells	250 mL
6 cups	chicken stock or canned broth	1.5 L
1	19 oz. (540 mL) can white kidney beans, drained	1

In a large pot, heat the oil and butter. Add the onion and leeks. Cover and cook gently until tender. Add the garlic and cook another minute. Add the tomatoes and tomato paste, and stir well. Add the carrots, celery, squash, parsley, oregano, basil, cayenne, black pepper, and macaroni shells. Stir in the chicken stock. Bring to a boil, reduce the heat, and cook until the macaroni is tender, about 30 minutes. Add the drained kidney beans and heat through. Serve hot.

HEARTY DOUBLE-MUSHROOM AND BARLEY SOUP

A big, steamy bowl of thick and hearty mushroom and barley soup is just the ticket on a fall evening—chunky with fresh sliced mushrooms, and enhanced with the addition of earthy-tasting dried mushrooms. Barley is a wonderful thickener for soups, producing a suave, velvety, rich result—full of nutrition, carbohydrates, and protein. Serves 6-8.

1 cup	pearl barley	250 mL
4 tbsp.	butter	60 mL
2 tbsp.	vegetable oil	30 mL
1	large onion, coarsely diced	1
1 tbsp.	sugar	15 mL
1 1/2 lbs.	fresh mushrooms, tightly capped and closed, wiped clean (do not wash), thinly sliced	750 g
6	large carrots, peeled and cut into large dice	6
1 oz.	dried mushrooms, soaked in warm water to cover 30 minutes, snipped into pieces with scissors	30 g
1 tsp.	salt	5 mL
1/2 tsp.	coarsely ground black pepper	2 mL
8 cups	chicken or beef stock	2 L
6 tbsp.	snipped fresh dill	90 mL
3-4 tbsp.	fresh lemon juice	45-60 mL
1 cup	sour cream	250 mL
2 tbsp.	snipped fresh chives	30 mL

Place the barley in a bowl and cover with simmering water. Soak for 30 minutes and drain.

In a large stock pot, heat the butter and oil over medium-high heat. Add the onion and sauté 5-6 minutes until translucent. Add the sugar and sauté 2 minutes to carmelize slightly. Add the sliced fresh mushrooms and carrots, and sauté 8-10 minutes longer, tossing the mushrooms quickly, until slightly golden on the edges.

Add the snipped soaked mushrooms with their soaking liquid, the drained barley, salt, pepper, and stock. Bring the mixture to a simmer, add 4 tbsp. (60 mL) of the dill, partially cover the pot, and simmer over medium-low heat about 1 1/2 hours.

Add the lemon juice, stir in the remaining 2 tbsp. (30 mL) dill, and taste and correct for seasonings. Simmer 5 minutes. Ladle into deep soup bowls. Top each serving with a dollop of sour cream and a sprinkling of snipped chives. Pass the pepper grinder!

LEEK, POTATO, AND PARSNIP CHOWDER

What could be more comforting and nourishing than a sweet, herby soup made of root vegetables? This one is a delicate, creamy concoction, perfect served in chunky bowls alongside a loaf of Irish Whole Wheat Soda Bread (p. 151). Serves 4.

2 tbsp.	margarine or butter	30 mL
1	large leek, chopped	1
3	medium potatoes, peeled and diced (about 3 cups (750 mL))	3
1	large parsnip, peeled and diced (about 1 1/2 cups (375 mL))	1
1 3/4 cups	chicken stock	425 mL
1	bay leaf	1
1/4 tsp.	dried thyme	1 mL
1 cup	milk	250 mL
8	slices bacon, chopped	8
	salt and pepper to taste	

In a medium saucepan, melt the margarine. Add the leek, potatoes, and parsnip, and sauté over medium-high heat, stirring, for 4 minutes. Pour in the stock and add the bay leaf and thyme. Reduce the heat to low, cover, and simmer 15 minutes until vegetables are cooked.

Remove the pan from the heat and with a fork, crush about half of the potato and parsnip against the sides of the pan to thicken the chowder. Return the pan to the heat, stir in the milk, and bring to a boil. Keep warm.

In a small pan, cook the bacon until crisp. Drain.

Remove the bay leaf from the chowder and discard. Season the soup to taste with salt and pepper. Sprinkle with bacon and serve.

SAVOURY CREAMED ONION SOUP

Here is a delicious twist on an old favourite—good old onion soup, but creamy and thick, and just a bit spicy. Serve it freshly prepared, piping hot, ladled out into deep crockery bowls. A handful of Dilled Matchstick Croutons (see p. 149) are perfect on top. All you need is a hot loaf of sourdough bread, a crock of butter, and baked apples with a cinnamon-flavoured syrup for dessert. Serves 6.

8 tbsp.	butter	120 g
2 quarts	thinly sliced onions, packed	2 L
1 tbsp.	sugar	15 mL
1 tsp.	paprika	5 mL
pinch	cayenne pepper	pinch
1/4 tsp.	*each* ground nutmeg and allspice	1 mL
1/3 cup	all-purpose flour	75 mL
1/3 cup	dry sherry	75 mL
1 tbsp.	fresh lemon juice	15 mL
2 cups	beef stock	500 mL
1 quart	milk	1 L
	salt and freshly ground black pepper to taste	
1-2 cups	whipping cream	250-500 mL
	Dilled Matchstick Croutons (see p. 149)	
	snipped fresh chives for garnish	

In a large stock pot, heat the butter until bubbly over medium heat. Add the onions, toss to coat, and sauté slowly about 40 minutes until softened and pale golden brown. Add the sugar after 30 minutes to help carmelize the onions. Stir in the paprika, cayenne, nutmeg, and allspice, increase the heat to medium-high, and cook until bubbly, about 2-3 minutes. Stir in the flour, sprinkling it slowly over the onions, and cook several minutes, stirring.

Add the sherry and cook 3-4 minutes. Stir in the lemon juice, beef stock, and milk, and bring the entire mixture to a simmer, stirring. Season with salt and black pepper. Simmer the soup, uncovered, 20 minutes to blend the flavours. Add the cream and simmer 10-15 minutes to heat through. Taste and correct for seasonings. Remove the soup from the heat, and let it rest 20 minutes before serving for the flavours to blend and the soup to thicken.

Serve the soup hot, each portion garnished with a handful of the croutons and a sprinkling of fresh chives.

CURRIED WINTER SQUASH AND APPLE BISQUE

This is a lovely soup to serve to guests—it is a gorgeous first course with its lovely pale orange colour and enticing aroma. The sprinkling of toasted walnuts adds a dressy and crunchy filip. Serve with fresh baked buttermilk biscuits. Serves 6.

6 tbsp.	butter	90 mL
1	large onion, minced	1
2	tart green (Newton or Granny Smith) apples, peeled, cored, and diced	2
2	butternut squash (about 3 lbs. (1.5 kg) total weight), peeled and cubed	2
2 tbsp.	brown sugar, packed	30 mL
1 tbsp.	curry powder	15 mL
1 tsp.	*each* ground ginger and salt	5 mL
1/2 tsp.	*each* ground mace, nutmeg, and allspice	2 mL
3 cups	chicken broth	750 mL
2 cups	apple cider (unfiltered)	500 mL
	freshly ground black and white pepper to taste	
2 tbsp.	fresh lemon juice	30 mL
1 cup	coarsely broken walnuts, toasted in a 325°F (160°C) oven 8-10 minutes, cooled	250 mL
	ground nutmeg or allspice to taste	

Heat the butter in a large stock pot over medium heat until bubbly. Add the minced onion and apples, and sauté until just softened, stirring. Add the cubed squash and stir-fry 2-3 minutes. Stir in the brown sugar, curry powder, ginger, salt, mace, nutmeg, and allspice. Sauté 2-3 minutes until bubbly. Add the chicken broth and bring the mixture to a simmer over medium heat. Partially cover the pot and simmer 45 minutes until the squash is very tender.

Purée the mixture, in several batches, in a food processor fitted with a steel blade. Return the purée to the pot and stir in the apple cider. Bring the mixture to a simmer, partially cover, and simmer 15 minutes. Grind in the peppercorns to taste and add the lemon juice. Heat the soup through for 10 minutes, uncovered. Serve piping hot, each serving sprinkled with a generous spoonful or two of toasted walnuts and a dusting of nutmeg or allspice.

UMPKIN BISQUE WITH CHILI

This savoury, creamy bisque is a delight—slightly sharp with the zip of chili powder, and fun to serve with a garnish of crisply fried strips of corn tortillas. Serve it with minced fresh cilantro and diced green onions, a hot loaf of cheese bread, and a platter of cold sliced Black Forest ham. Serves 4-6.

2 tbsp.	butter	30 mL
1 tbsp.	corn oil	15 mL
1	medium onion, diced	1
2	stalks celery, diced	2
1	red bell pepper, diced	1
1 tbsp.	brown sugar, packed	15 mL
1 1/2 tsp.	chili powder	7 mL
1/4 tsp.	ground cumin	1 mL
1/4 tsp.	ground cloves	1 mL
1 1/2 cups	cooked puréed pumpkin (fresh or canned)	375 mL
12 oz.	dark Mexican beer	375 mL
2 1/2 cups	chicken stock	625 mL
	(or 2 10 oz. (284 mL) cans)	
1 tbsp.	cider vinegar	15 mL
4-5 dashes	bottled hot pepper sauce	4-5 dashes
	salt and freshly ground black pepper to taste	
	corn oil for frying	
3	6 inch (15 cm) corn tortillas, cut in half and julienned into 1/4 inch (6 mm) strips	3
4-6 tbsp.	snipped fresh cilantro	60-90 mL
1/2 cup	thinly sliced green onions	125 mL

In a deep stock pot, heat the butter and the 1 tbsp. (15 mL) corn oil over medium-high heat until bubbling. Add the onion, celery, and red pepper, and sauté until translucent and pale golden on the edges. Add the brown sugar, chili powder, cumin, and cloves, and sauté 2-3 minutes to flavour the vegetables.

Stir in the pumpkin, beer, and broth. Bring the mixture to a simmer, reduce the heat to medium, partially cover, and simmer 1 hour. Stir in the vinegar, hot pepper sauce, salt, and pepper, and simmer 30 minutes longer, uncovered. Set the soup aside, partially covered, to keep it hot. It should be creamy and thick.

Pour corn oil in a non-stick skillet to a depth of 1 inch (2.5 cm) and heat over medium-high heat. The oil is ready when a strip of tortilla dropped into the pan floats to the top immediately (the frying temperature should be about 375°F [190°C]). Fry the tortilla strips, in several batches, 2-3 minutes until crispy and golden brown. Remove the strips with a slotted spoon or mesh strainer as they crisp, and drain on absorbent paper. To serve the soup, ladle into wide, shallow bowls. Top each serving with a small handful of crisp tortilla strips, 1 tbsp. (15 mL) snipped cilantro, and a sprinkling of green onions. Serve at once, piping hot.

The East Gourmet features a photograph of this recipe on page 143.

HARVEST ORANGE SPICE PUMPKIN SOUP

This lovely pumpkin soup is a delicious prelude to a fall supper, served up in pretty shallow soup bowls or even hollowed-out miniature pumpkins, each serving garnished with a thin slice of orange and a sprinkling of cinnamon-spiced croutons. Follow the soup course with a succulent roast loin of pork, fresh green beans with garlic butter, and real mashed potatoes. Big bowls of chocolate ice cream and thin ginger cookies make a perfect dessert. Serves 4-6.

2 tbsp.	butter	30 mL
1	medium onion, diced	1
1 tbsp.	brown sugar, packed	15 mL
1/4 tsp.	ground cinnamon	1 mL
1/4 tsp.	ground mace	1 mL
3/4 tsp.	ground ginger	3 mL
1/4 tsp.	ground allspice	1 mL
1/2 tsp.	*each* salt and freshly ground black pepper	2 mL
1	14 oz. (398 mL) can puréed pumpkin	1
1 cup	fresh orange juice	250 mL
2 tsp.	freshly grated orange rind	10 mL
2 cups	rich chicken stock	500 mL
1 cup	whipping cream or half-and-half cream	250 mL
	thin julienne strips orange rind for garnish (optional)	
	Cinnamon Spiced Croutons (recipe follows)	

Heat the butter in a deep soup pot over medium heat until bubbling, and add the onion. Sauté, stirring, until softened and slightly golden. Add the brown sugar, cinnamon, mace, ginger, allspice, salt, and pepper, and sauté the mixture 2-3 minutes until glossy.

Stir in the puréed pumpkin, orange juice, grated orange rind, and chicken stock. Bring the mixture to a simmer, partially cover, and simmer 45 minutes to blend the flavours. Whisk in the cream and heat 30 minutes longer. Taste and correct for salt and seasonings.

Ladle the soup into warmed, shallow soup bowls, and garnish each serving with thin slices of orange rind and a generous handful of crisp, warm croutons. Pass the pepper grinder!

CINNAMON SPICED CROUTONS

3 tbsp.	*each* butter and vegetable or olive oil	45 mL
1 1/2 cups	bakery-style white bread, crusts removed, cut into 1/2 inch (1 cm) dice, air-dried several hours to firm	375 mL
	ground cinnamon and paprika to taste	
	salt and freshly ground black pepper to taste	

Heat the butter and oil in a large non-stick skillet over medium-high heat until sizzling. Add the diced bread, and sauté the croutons, stirring, until golden brown and crispy, about 5-7 minutes. During the final minute, sprinkle evenly to taste with cinnamon, paprika, salt, and pepper. Set the skillet aside 20 minutes to cool before serving. These croutons are best served within several hours of preparation.

The Easy Gourmet features a photograph of this recipe on page 143.

CREAM OF CHESTNUT AND MUSHROOM SOUP

This creamy, distinctively flavoured chestnut soup can be served at any time of year—canned chestnuts make it simple, fresh shallots and cream make it elegant. For a decorative finish, swirl a little whipping cream on top of each serving. Serves 8.

3 tbsp.	margarine or butter	45 mL
12 oz.	mushrooms, sliced	375 g
2	shallots, finely chopped	2
1	10 oz. (284 mL) can chicken broth	1
1	10 oz. (284 mL) can water	1
1	15 oz. (425 g) can whole chestnuts in water	1
1	14 oz. (398 mL) can tomatoes	1
dash	*each* bottled hot pepper and Worcestershire sauce	dash
1 cup	half-and-half cream	250 mL
2 tbsp.	chopped fresh parsley	30 mL
	salt and pepper to taste	
	whipping cream and chopped fresh parsley for garnish	

Melt the margarine in a large saucepan. Add the mushrooms and shallots, and sauté over medium heat for 10 minutes, stirring occasionally. Pour in the chicken broth and water. Bring to a boil. Place the chestnuts in a sieve and rinse under cold running water. Drain and chop the chestnuts. Add the chestnuts and tomatoes to the pan, reduce the heat, and simmer for 5 minutes. Add the hot pepper and Worcestershire sauce.

Purée the mixture well in batches in a food processor or blender. Return the soup to the pan and add the cream. Heat through over medium heat, stir in the parsley, and season to taste with salt and pepper. Pour into soup bowls, swirl a little whipping cream into the centre of each serving, sprinkle with parsley, and serve.

Opposite: (top to bottom) Pumpkin Bisque with Chili (p.138), Harvest Orange Spice Pumpkin Soup (p.140).

RUSSELS SPROUT SOUP

A generous garnish of toasted almonds is the final touch to this nourishing, delicately flavoured soup made from brussels sprouts, the best of cool weather vegetables. The soup also freezes well—so handy for last-minute heating in the microwave! Serves 4-6.

1	large onion, chopped	1
1/2 lb.	potatoes, chopped	250 g
3 tbsp.	butter	45 mL
2 lbs.	brussels sprouts	1 kg
4 cups	chicken stock	1 L
	salt and freshly ground black pepper to taste	
1/2 tsp.	grated nutmeg	2 mL
1/2 cup	whipping cream	125 mL
6 tbsp.	flaked almonds	90 mL

In a 12 cup (3 L) microproof casserole dish, place the onion, potatoes and 2 tbsp. (30 mL) of the butter. Cover and microwave on HIGH 100% power 3-5 minutes until the vegetables are softened, stirring at least once during the cooking time.

Wash the brussels sprouts, trim the ends, and cut each in half. Add to the casserole dish. Cover and microwave on HIGH 100% power 6-8 minutes until the sprouts are soft. Blend in the chicken stock.

Purée until smooth. Return to the microwave, cover, and cook on HIGH 100% power to bring to a boil. Season to taste with salt and pepper. (The soup may be cooled and frozen at this point.)

Blend in the nutmeg and microwave at HIGH 100% power to bring to a boil. Blend in the cream.

Place the almonds and the remaining 1 tbsp. (15 mL) butter in a small microproof dish. Microwave on HIGH 100% power in 1 minute increments until the almonds are golden brown, stirring after each cooking period.

Sprinkle toasted almonds over the hot soup and serve.

FRESH TOMATO SOUP WITH BACON AND CROUTONS

Fresh tomato soup, especially at summer's end or early fall, is a treat indeed. Succulent, meaty fresh tomatoes will produce the most delicious soup. Quickly prepared, this soup is lovely served up in deep crockery bowls, each serving topped with crisp bacon and basil-flavoured sourdough croutons. Serves 6.

4 lbs.	fresh tomatoes	2 kg
3 tbsp.	olive oil	45 mL
1	medium onion, diced	1
2	large cloves garlic, crushed	2
1 tbsp.	sugar	15 mL
3-4 cups	beef or chicken broth	750 mL-1 L
1 tsp.	salt, or to taste	10 mL
1 tsp.	cracked black pepper	5 mL
1/2 cup	lightly packed fresh basil, stacked and cut into ultra-thin ribbons	125 mL
1/2 lb.	sliced bacon, fried until crisp and coarsely crumbled (prepare no more than 15 minutes before serving to ensure the bacon stays warm and crispy)	250 g
	Sourdough Basil Croutons (recipe follows)	

Plunge the tomatoes into boiling water 15-30 seconds, remove, and rinse with cold water. The skins will pull off very easily, in one piece, when started with the tip of a sharp paring knife. Discard the skins and core the tomatoes.

Heat the olive oil in a large, deep saucepan and add the diced onion. Sauté 5-6 minutes until slightly softened and pale golden at the edges. Add the garlic and sauté 1-2 minutes to flavour the onions. Add the prepared tomatoes and sauté 6-7 minutes, stirring. Stir in the sugar, add the broth, salt, and pepper, and bring the mixture to a simmer. Partially cover the soup and cook 1 hour. The tomatoes should be very pulpy and soft.

In small batches, purée the soup to a slightly chunky and grainy purée (do not purée smooth). Return the soup to the pot and heat through over medium heat. Taste and correct for seasonings, and stir in the fresh basil ribbons. Heat the soup through for 2-3 minutes before serving.

Serve the soup hot or warm, each bowl topped with warm, crispy bacon and freshly prepared Sourdough Basil Croutons.

SOURDOUGH BASIL CROUTONS

1/3 cup	olive oil	75 mL
3 cups	day-old sourdough bread, crusts on, cut into 1/2 inch (1 cm) cubes and air-dried several hours or overnight	750 mL
	garlic seasoning salt to taste	
3-4 tsp.	dried basil, crumbled	15-20 mL
	freshly ground black pepper to taste	

Heat the olive oil in a very large non-stick skillet over medium heat. Add the cubed bread, toss at once to coat with the olive oil, and fry 7-8 minutes, tossing, until golden brown and crispy. Season with the garlic salt, basil, and pepper, and heat 1-2 minutes longer. Set the skillet aside and cool the croutons. Serve within 3-4 hours for the best flavour.

AST COAST CHEDDAR SOUP

Cheddar cheese soup is just the ticket on a cool, crisp evening, welcoming all to the table for a bowl of savoury, soul-satisfying soup. Serve with a loaf of hot, crisp sourdough bread, grilled knockwurst and mustard, and a wooden bowl brimming with crisp fall apples and walnuts in the shell. Serves 6.

4 tbsp.	butter	60 mL
1 cup	*each* finely minced carrot, celery, and onion	250 g
4 tbsp.	all-purpose flour	60 mL
pinch	*each* ground nutmeg, allspice, and cloves	pinch
1 tbsp.	dry English-style mustard	15 mL
2 cups	chicken stock	500 g
1 quart	milk	1 L
1 lb.	sharp Canadian cheddar cheese, coarsely shredded	500 g
1 cup	whipping cream, heated to warm	250 g
	freshly ground black pepper to taste	
	several dashes Worcestershire sauce (optional)	
	several drops bottled hot pepper sauce (optional)	
	Dilled Matchstick Croutons (recipe follows)	

Heat the butter in a large stock pot over medium heat until bubbly. Add the minced carrot, celery, and onion, and sauté, stirring, until the vegetables are softened, translucent, and pale golden. Sift in the flour, nutmeg, allspice, cloves, and dry mustard, and cook with the vegetables until bubbly, about 3 minutes. Whisk in the chicken stock and bring the mixture to a simmer. Partially cover and simmer 20 minutes.

Add the milk and bring gently to a simmer. Gradually, in small handfuls, add the shredded cheese, stirring to melt each batch before adding more. When all the cheese has melted, add the heated cream. Season to taste with pepper, Worcestershire, and hot pepper sauce, and heat through until piping hot. Serve in shallow crockery soup bowls, each topped with a generous handful of Dilled Matchstick Croutons.

DILLED MATCHSTICK CROUTONS

3 tbsp.	*each* butter and vegetable oil	45 mL
3 cups	(measure after cutting) firm white bread, crusts removed, cut into matchsticks (1/4 x 1 1/2 inches (6 mm x 4 cm)), air-dried several hours or overnight	750 mL
I tbsp.	dried dill	15 mL
	ground nutmeg and seasoning salt to taste	

Heat the butter and oil in a very large non-stick skillet over medium heat until bubbly and sizzling. Add the bread and toss quickly to coat. Fry 6-8 minutes, tossing, until golden brown and crispy. Season during the last minute or two with the dill, a light sprinkling of nutmeg, and seasoning salt to taste. Set the skillet aside and allow the croutons to cool completely. Serve within several hours of preparation for best flavour.

BREADS

Made for autumn weather—and autumn appetites—the bread recipes in this section are lovely accompaniments to any soup or entrée in this book. Cranberry-Orange Bread and Zucchini Bread take advantage of fresh seasonal produce, and Apricot-Raisin Muffins or Batter Corn Bread are hits both at dinner and in lunch boxes the next day.

BATTER CORN BREAD

Jalapeño peppers give a south-of-the-border bite to this easy yeast bread, a natural accompaniment to Tuna Casserole With a Twist (p. 75) or a pot roast. Makes 2 medium loaves.

1/2 cup	buttermilk	125 mL
1 tsp.	sugar	5 mL
1 1/2 tbsp.	dry yeast	20 mL
4 tbsp.	oil	60 mL
2	eggs	2
1	14 oz. (398 mL) can cream-style corn	1
2-4	jalapeño chile peppers, seeded and finely chopped	2-4
1/2	medium onion, finely chopped	1/2
pinch	salt	pinch
1 1/2 cups	grated cheddar cheese	375 mL
1/2 cup + 3 tbsp.	corn meal	170 mL
3 cups	all-purpose flour	750 mL

Heat the buttermilk to lukewarm and stir in the sugar. Add the yeast and let stand 5-10 minutes to soften.

In a large bowl mix together the oil, eggs, corn, peppers, onion, salt, cheese, and 1/2 cup (125 mL) of the corn meal. Stir in the softened yeast.

Stir in the flour, 1 cup (250 mL) at a time, until the mixture pulls away from the sides of the bowl but is still very sticky. Leave it in the mixing bowl and place, covered, in a warm place to rise, about 1 hour.

Grease 2 bread or loaf pans, 8 x 4 x 3 inches (20 x 10 x 8 cm), and sprinkle each one with 1 tbsp. (15 mL) of the remaining corn meal.

Stir down the risen sponge and divide between the 2 pans. Sprinkle the tops with the remaining 1 tbsp. (15 mL) corn meal. Let rise in a warm place for 20-25 minutes, uncovered.

Heat the oven to 375°F (190°C). Bake the bread 40-50 minutes or until the top is dark golden brown and the bottom sounds hollow when tapped.

Cut into thick slices and serve warm.

The Easy Gourmet features a photograph of this recipe on page 89.

I RISH WHOLE WHEAT SODA BREAD

The beauty of this traditional Irish quick bread is how fast and easy it is to make. Since it has no yeast or any other preservatives, it should be eaten as soon as it is baked. Its distinctive flavour makes it a perfect accompaniment to winter soups, or cut it into wedges at lunchtime and serve it with an assortment of cheeses. Makes 1 loaf.

2 1/2 cups	all-purpose flour	625 mL
1 cup	whole wheat flour	250 mL
4 tbsp.	quick-cooking oats	60 mL
4 tbsp.	bran	60 mL
2 tsp.	sugar	10 mL
2 tsp.	baking soda	10 mL
1 tsp.	salt	5 mL
1 3/4 cups	buttermilk	425 mL
1/2 tbsp.	melted butter or margarine	7 mL
1/2 tbsp.	quick-cooking rolled oats	7 mL

Heat the oven to 400°F (200°C).

In a large bowl, combine the flours, quick-cooking oats, bran, sugar, baking soda, and salt. Pour in the buttermilk and mix with a knife to make a soft, slightly sticky dough. Do not overmix. Roughly form into a ball and place the dough on a lightly floured surface. Knead lightly a maximum of 12 times (overkneading will toughen the bread). Form into a round about 7 inches (17.5 cm) in diameter and about 1 inch (2.5 cm) thick.

Place the loaf on a greased cookie sheet and score a deep cross in the top with a sharp knife. Brush it with the melted butter and sprinkle with the quick-cooking rolled oats. Bake about 30 minutes, until light golden brown. Serve warm.

The Easy Gourmet features a photograph of this recipe on page 125.

SAVOURY BISCUIT RING

So quick and easy to make, this side dish is as gorgeous to look at as it is delicious to eat. Serve it warm next to almost any main course—fish, poultry, meat from the barbecue, salad, pasta, or even all by itself! Serves 6-8.

4 tbsp.	butter	60 mL
2 tbsp.	mixed dried herbs	30 mL
2	4 oz. (125 g) pkgs. refrigerated buttermilk biscuits	2
1 cup	finely chopped cooked ham (about 4 oz. (125 g))	250 mL
4 tbsp.	finely chopped garlic dill pickle	60 mL
2 tbsp.	Dijon mustard	30 mL

Place the butter in a 10 inch (25 cm) microproof tube pan. Microwave on HIGH 100% power 45 seconds-1 minute until melted. Stir in the herbs.

Separate the refrigerated biscuits and cut each biscuit in half horizontally. Place half the biscuit pieces in a circle on the butter and herb mixture in the tube pan, overlapping the biscuits slightly.

Mix together the chopped ham, garlic pickle, and Dijon mustard. Spread evenly over the biscuits in the pan. Top with the remaining biscuit halves, arranged in a circle and slightly overlapping.

Microwave on HIGH 100% power 6-8 minutes, rotating the pan halfway through the cooking time if necessary.

Let stand, uncovered, 3-4 minutes.

Invert the pan onto a serving plate. Let the pan stand over the ring for a few seconds to allow the butter topping to drizzle over the biscuits.

Cut in wedges and serve warm.

CRANBERRY-ORANGE BREAD

Fresh cranberries and tangy-sweet orange juice give this bread a full, delicious flavour, and they keep it moist and tender. Slice it up to accompany a festive dinner of chicken or turkey, or serve it with butter at afternoon tea, or pack slices into the family's lunch boxes. Makes 8 mini-loaves or 2 medium loaves.

1 tbsp.	dry yeast	15 mL
2 tbsp.	sugar	30 mL
1/2 cup	very warm water	125 mL
1/2 cup	fresh orange juice (approx. 3 small oranges)	125 mL
1 cup	evaporated milk	250 mL
2 tbsp.	melted butter	30 mL
1-2 tsp.	salt	5-10 mL
	rind of 1 orange, finely chopped	
1 cup	fresh or frozen cranberries, coarsely chopped	250 mL
1 1/2 cups	graham flour	375 mL
3 cups	all-purpose flour	750 mL

Dissolve the yeast and sugar in the warm water and orange juice. Let stand until softened.

In a large bowl, combine the evaporated milk, butter, salt, orange rind, and cranberries. Add the dissolved yeast. Stir in the graham flour and beat well.

Add the white flour, 1 cup (250 mL) at a time, until the dough pulls away from the sides of the bowl. Turn out onto a floured surface and knead, adding more flour as necessary, until the dough is smooth. It will still be a little sticky.

Place the dough in a greased bowl and let stand, covered, in a warm place for about 1 hour. Turn out onto a floured surface and shape into 8 mini-loaves or 2 medium loaves. Place in greased loaf pans and let rise until the dough is about 1 inch (2.5 cm) above the edge of the pan, about 15-20 minutes.

Heat the oven to 375°F (190°C) and bake the bread until the loaves are well risen and golden brown, and sound hollow when tapped on the bottom, about 30 minutes.

APRICOT-RAISIN MUFFINS

Those who like their muffins fruity and full of crunch and flavour will find these perfect for breakfast, lunch, or snacks. The muffins freeze well, so make an extra batch and keep some on hand for lunchboxes. Makes 12 .

1/2 cup	dried apricots	125 mL
1 1/2 cups	all-purpose flour	375 mL
3/4 cup	whole wheat flour	175 mL
4 tbsp.	quick-cooking oats	60 mL
1/2 cup	brown sugar, packed	125 mL
2 1/2 tsp.	baking powder	12 mL
1/4 tsp.	salt	1 mL
1/3 cup	chopped walnuts	75 mL
4 tbsp.	dark raisins	60 mL
2	eggs	2
1 cup	buttermilk	250 mL
1/2 cup	melted butter or margarine	125 mL
2 tbsp.	honey	30 mL
1 tsp.	grated orange rind	5 mL

Place the dried apricots in a small bowl and cover with plenty of cold water. Soak 3-4 hours. Drain off the water and chop the apricots.

Heat the oven to 400°F (200°C). Line a deep muffin pan with large paper muffin cups.

In a large bowl, combine the flours, oats, brown sugar, baking powder, and salt. Stir in the apricots, walnuts, and raisins. In a small bowl, beat the eggs. Stir in the buttermilk, butter, honey, and orange rind. Pour this into the flour mixture and fold in very lightly. Do not overmix. Divide the mixture evenly among the muffin cups. Bake 25-35 minutes, or until risen and pale golden on top.

APPLE-NUT SPICE MUFFINS

Substitute 1 cup (250 mL) coarsely grated apple for the apricots. Omit the grated orange rind and stir 1 tsp. (5 mL) ground cinnamon into the flour mixture instead. Before baking, sprinkle with a mixture of 1 tbsp. (15 mL) sugar and 1/4 tsp. (1 mL) ground cinnamon.

Z UCCHINI BREAD

Flecks of succulent fresh zucchini make this quick bread as gorgeous as it is delicious. Serve thick wedges with cream cheese and fruit, as part of a light dinner with soup and salad, or all by itself. It is best eaten the day it is made, or freeze it as soon as it is cooled. Makes 2 loaves.

2 cups	whole wheat flour	500 mL
1 cup	all-purpose flour	250 mL
1/2 cup	dark brown sugar, lightly packed	125 mL
2 tbsp.	wheat germ	30 mL
1 tbsp.	baking powder	15 mL
1 1/2 tsp.	baking soda	7 mL
1 tsp.	salt	5 mL
2 cups	buttermilk	500 mL
1	medium zucchini, grated and squeezed dry	1

Heat the oven to 325°F (160°C). Grease two 8 x 4 x 3 inch (20 x 10 x 8 cm) loaf pans.

Mix together the whole wheat and white flours, brown sugar, wheat germ, baking powder, baking soda, and salt.

Stir together the buttermilk and zucchini.

Add the wet ingredients to the dry ingredients, stirring gently until just moistened. Spoon the batter into the prepared pans and bake 50-60 minutes or until a toothpick inserted just off centre comes out clean.

Let the bread cool in the pans.

INDEX